THE WANNABE INVESTOR

THE WANNABE INVESTOR

40 Must-Know Facts Before Buying Your First Stock

ANN MARIE SABATH

SONCATA PRESS

NEW YORK, NEW YORK

This edition first published in 2024 by Soncata Press LLC.
With offices at:
    340 W 57th Street, Suite 2C
    New York, New York 10019
    www.soncatapress.com

Hardback ISBN: 979-8-9898574-1-8
Paperback ISBN: 979-8-9898574-2-5
ebook ISBN: 979-8-9898574-0-1
Audiobook ISBN: 979-8-9898574-3-2

Library of Congress Cataloging-in-Publication Data available upon request.

This publication is designed to provide accurate and authoritative information in regards the subject matter covered. It is sold with the understanding that neither the author nor the publisher is engaged in rendering legal, accounting, securities trading, tax, or other professional services. If legal advice or other expert assistance is required, the services of a competent person should be sought.

Cover design by Howard Grossman.

Attention Educational Institutions and Businesses:
Soncata Press books are available at special quantity discounts with bulk purchase for educational, business, or sales promotional use. For information, please write to contact@soncatapress.com.

To Allan, whose unwavering guidance over the past decade has illuminated my path in the world of investing. I'm grateful for the wealth of knowledge and wisdom you've imparted to me from your own sixty-five-year journey in the market.

Contents

Introduction

An investment in knowledge pays the best interest.
BENJAMIN FRANKLIN, AMERICAN FOUNDING FATHER

———————
———————

This book has been a long time coming—thirty-one years to be exact.

Back in 1992, I was among the roughly 40 percent of Americans who did not have money invested in the stock market.[1] However, my small business had finally succeeded to the point where I had some money I *could* invest, so I worked with a financial advisor for a couple of years. Fortunately for him, he was promoted to work with clients whose portfolios were in the seven-figure range. Unfortunately for me, I was not one of them. My portfolio was pawned off on a less-seasoned advisor who had just earned her Certified Financial Planner (CFP) designation. For a while, I was content having her manage my portfolio, but then her assistant became my go-to person. That was the proverbial straw that broke the camel's back—and our working relationship.

I closed my account with that investment firm and—with no real investing knowledge of my own—thought my best option was to transfer my funds into safe, simple certificates of deposit (CDs). That's where I left my money for the next twenty years.

Although I read many investing books during the time my money was growing at lethargic rates in those CDs, the language of Wall Street remained a foreign tongue to me. I thought joining an investment club might give me a better education. While I made two lifelong friends from the group, even after listening to other members give their stock valuation reports, I still struggled to understand the ins and outs of investing.

It took a long time before I got brave enough to start *really* learning about the stock market. One key to that change: I met Allan, who soon became my personal "Warren Buffett" and set me on the road to investing—something he himself had been doing for more than fifty years. He helped me get a grasp on the topic, assured me that it was easier to invest than I thought, and coached me through my first few investments.

While it's been fantastic to have an investment guru for the past ten-plus years, if I'd been able to find an investment book in down-to-earth English earlier, perhaps I could have cured my financial illiteracy and put my money to work decades sooner . . .

The Wannabe Investor is the investing primer that I wish I'd had all those years ago. I wrote it to be an easy-to-understand guide to the basics of investing *for you.* Drawing from my own experience, I took big chunks of information that I knew could be intimidating and unwieldy and broke them down into easy-to-understand tidbits—forty must-know facts, ranging from simple definitions to common mistakes. And throughout, I've shared many "Allanisms"—pieces of advice my investing guru has given me over the years that have helped me succeed. Some are ideas he picked up from other wise investors; others are mantras he created himself.

If you're reading this book and haven't yet started investing in the market, what has been holding you back? Chances are, it might be one of these reasons:

- You're living paycheck to paycheck.
- You have student debt that you want to finish paying off before you start putting money in the market.
- You think you don't have enough money set aside to start investing.

- You're not sure how to open a brokerage account.
- You want your money to be easily accessible, so you keep it in the bank.
- You consider putting money in the stock market to be too much like gambling, and you're not ready to take that kind of risk.
- You don't have the necessary knowledge—yet.

If you can relate to one or more of these reasons, I promise you: *The Wannabe Investor* is for you—and in Must-Know Fact 1, we'll address each of these points.

After reading *The Wannabe Investor*, if you choose to invest independently, you'll have tools to make more effective choices. In fact, pages 214 to 217 have been dedicated exclusively for you to transition to going from being a wannabe investor to a first-time investor. If you decide to work with a financial advisor, you'll have acquired the knowledge to better understand what they are explaining to you and doing on your behalf. Either way, my hope is that this book will assist you in making better decisions for your financial future.

To be clear, ***I am not a financial advisor***. I'm an ordinary person who learned what seemed to me an extraordinary thing. As a result, I was able to greatly increase not only my knowledge but also my portfolio account balance. If I can do it, so can you.

Are you ready? Then let's get started!

Ann Marie Sabath

Wait! Before You Buy a Single Share...

Live within your income and save so that you can invest.
CHARLIE MUNGER, FORMER VICE CHAIRMAN OF
BERKSHIRE HATHAWAY

———————
————

Before you start investing, it's important to understand a few basics about your relationship with money. Just as our relationships differ among friends and family members, each of us has our own relationship with money.

Some people live according to the "law of scarcity," which can lead them to panic about money when they lack it and yet burn through it quickly when a windfall arrives. Others live according to the "law of abundance," which helps them remain calm and patient with their finances. The kind of relationship you have with money makes a significant difference in how your money grows.

Until I was in my thirties, I didn't think much about this relationship. I patterned my relationship with money after that of my parents: I made money by earning a living; I spent money paying bills (and on some frivolous things); and I saved money for unexpected expenses.

To me, money was a tool for taking care of my immediate financial responsibilities. I always thought there would be time down the line to plan for my financial future. However, after reading about the four Laws of Wealth in Phil Laut's book *Money Is My Friend*,[2] I realized I needed to reassess my relationship with money.

Laut's four laws are simple:

- The Earning Law: All human wealth is created by the human mind.
- The Spending Law: The value of money is determined by the buyer and seller in every transaction.
- The Saving Law: Savings is the accumulation of a surplus from your income.
- The Investing Law: Investing is spending capital in your name for the purpose of increasing your income.

Most of us apply the Earning Law and Spending Law, because we earn money by working and spend it on the things we need—food, clothing, shelter, and all the little things we think we must have. Some people have mastered the Saving Law better than others have; in my thirties, I was one of those who fritter away what they think is expendable income. Did you notice that you must follow the first three laws to get to the Investing Law? We must earn enough and not spend too much in order to save and thus have the opportunity to invest.

How do you think you're doing with the Saving Law? What about the Investing Law?

Before you start thinking about buying a single share of stock, make sure you have the following basics in place:

First, if your employer offers a 401(k) or similar retirement plan, participate in it. Employer-sponsored retirement accounts such as 401(k)s or 403(b)s are among the easiest ways to grow your money for your financial future, especially if you start contributing early and continue to do so regularly. These plans offer you the chance to make pretax contributions to your account, meaning the government doesn't take its cut of that money until you withdraw it in retirement; typically, the money is automatically deducted from your paycheck, so the process is practically effortless; and employers often match employee contributions, essentially offering free money.

A common formula employers use is to provide a 50 percent match on funds you contribute, up to a set percentage of your salary—usually in the range of 4 to 6 percent. Let's say you earn $60,000 a year, and your employer provides a 50 percent match on up to 6 percent of your wages. That means if you contribute $3,600 of your pretax wages to your 401(k), your employer will contribute an additional $1,800. When was the last time someone offered you $1,800 for free? Of course, you can contribute more—up to the allowed maximum (which changes annually)—but at a minimum, be sure to contribute enough to get the full employer match!

Around half of US workers have the option of contributing to such a plan, and if you're one of them, I hope you are also among the four out of ten of those eligible who choose to participate. If your employer doesn't offer a retirement plan, or if you're self-employed, other tax-advantaged options are available, such as an individual 401(k) or an individual retirement account (IRA). In this case, I strongly recommend getting advice from your tax advisor or financial professional, due to the rules and limitations on these plans.

Regardless of which types of tax-advantaged accounts or plans you choose, the sooner you start, the more you will benefit in the long run. Because when it comes to the Investing Law, time is your greatest asset.

Now, it is true that putting money into your 401(k) is, without question, investing. However, what goes on in an employer-sponsored retirement plan is not precisely the type of investing this book will focus on. Historically, participants have not been able to invest in specific stocks through a 401(k)—just mutual funds and exchange-traded funds (ETFs), assets that we will discuss in detail later. In some ways, those options can be limiting, so *The Wannabe Investor* is intended to expand your options by sharing what you need to know to start investing in individual stocks and other assets outside your 401(k).

Second, build your emergency fund. While I certainly wouldn't wish it on you, if you lost your job tomorrow, would you have enough money saved to pay your bills while you searched for another? According to the Bureau of Labor Statistics,[3] in December 2023, the average amount of time a person remained unemployed in the US was about twenty-two weeks, or about five and a half months. The median was just over two months, meaning half of unemployed job seekers took less time than that to find their next job; half took more. Could you go two months—or five months or ten months—without a job?

There are many other kinds of emergencies that can interrupt your income or demand you lay out more than usual in a given month as well—household repair bills, medical emergencies, unforeseen travel. To deal with those surprises without sinking yourself in high-interest debt (think credit card debt), an emergency fund is vital.

There is no magic number for the "right" size emergency fund, but experts recommend setting aside *at minimum* enough to cover three to six months of your recurring expenses.

Third, pay off credit card debt. A Bankrate survey published in early 2023 found that 35 percent of US adults were carrying credit card balances from month to month.[4] Every day your high-interest credit card debt goes unpaid, it's costing you *a lot* of money!

If you are carrying balances on your credit cards, start paying them down. There are two popular methods for doing so:

- The "avalanche method," in which you pay the minimum on all cards and apply any extra funds toward the card with the highest interest rate. Once that card is paid off, you move to pay off the one with the next highest interest rate.
- The "snowball method," in which you pay the minimum on all cards and apply any extra funds toward the card with the *smallest balance*. Once that one is paid off, you move to the card with the next lowest balance.

I prefer the avalanche method because you end up paying less in total interest, but some people prefer the feeling of relief that comes with quickly extinguishing a debt. The two methods are similar roads to the same destination, so if you have credit card debt, pick the one that better suits your personality and get started.

If you carry high-interest revolving credit debt *and* lack an emergency fund (as many people do), you might be wondering which issue to tackle first.

Sallie Krawcheck, co-founder of the woman-centric digital investing platform Ellevest, believes that while having an emergency fund is essential, you shouldn't delay paying off credit card debt to build up that cushion.[5] The extra costs you'll pay on those credit card balances are just too high—and they've been getting higher. In September 2022, the average interest rate on a US credit card was about 16%; in September 2023, the average rate was around 21%. That's higher than it has been since the Fed started tracking rates in 1994.[6] Even if you're paying a lower-than-average rate, chances are you'll still be better off getting out from under those debts as quickly as possible.

Now, with the preliminaries out of the way, let's get to some facts!

ALLANISM

It's not how much you earn that determines your financial success; it's how you allocate your money.

MUST-KNOW FACT 1
Financial literacy is crucial for achieving economic stability and building wealth.

You wanna build your IQ higher in the next two years?
Be uncomfortable. That means, learn something
where you have a beginner's mind.
NOLAN BUSHNELL, FOUNDER OF ATARI

———————
———————

Financial literacy means having skills and knowledge related to money. It includes concepts such as budgeting, making spending decisions, and investing. With inadequate financial literacy, we may spend too much, save too little, make poor financing decisions, or become more susceptible to fraud—simply from not knowing how money works. According to the National Financial Educators Council, respondents to a 2023 survey reported that a lack of personal finance knowledge cost them an average of over $1,500 that year.[7]

Financial illiteracy hinders us from achieving financial stability, let alone building wealth.

Unfortunately, in the US, we do a lackluster job teaching financial literacy to our children. As of August 2023, only twenty-three states required high school students to take a personal finance course before graduation.[8] (Compare that to Denmark, which is tied with Sweden and Norway for the highest rate of financial literacy in the world and makes financial education mandatory for seventh, eighth, and ninth graders.[9]) That could improve soon: in 2023, forty-one states as well as Puerto Rico and the District of Columbia had some sort of legislation on the table related to teaching financial literacy.[10] However, those of us past high school age may still need to educate ourselves about money.

One of the most consistent ways of building wealth is to invest regularly and smartly in the stock market. The US stock market, as measured by the Standard & Poor's 500 index (S&P 500) since it was introduced in 1957, has shown annual growth averaging 10.7% (and just over 12% for the past decade[11]), far above what you could expect from a savings account or CD. And yet, as noted in the introduction to this book, about 40 percent of Americans don't invest in the stock market at all, which we know is at least partly due to lack of financial literacy.

Here are seven common reasons people give for not being in the market. Note whether you see yourself in any of them.

I'm living paycheck to paycheck. Many individuals can hardly pay their bills, let alone invest in the market. But if you have any disposable income in your budget, it's worth looking for ways you can trim your spending to find money to put toward your future. Now, this is not a book on budgeting. I'm not here to tell you to live frugally, nor to suggest you cut all the little pleasures out of your life. Nobody wants to hear another Boomer tell them that if they just give up their pricey coffee drinks, they'll soon be on the road to financial security. More importantly, people who try to make those kinds of harsh lifestyle changes often find them unsustainable. How you adjust your budget to find some cash to invest will involve choices that are personal to you. What matters more is having a big-picture, long-term mindset instead of one that's focused on instant gratification.

I have student debt I need to pay off before investing. Interest rates vary based on the type of loan, the amount financed, and the loan period. While interest rates on some student loans can exceed 10%, on others they may be in the low single digits. If you have a higher rate, you may want to pay it off sooner, much as you would high-interest credit card debt. However, if you have a lower interest rate, it can be wiser to invest any extra funds in the market rather than putting them toward retiring your student debt faster. If the market can earn you, say, 7% and your student loan rate is 3%, you effectively lose 4% by putting extra money toward your loan. (That 4% differential is known as your *opportunity cost*.) As a side note, the Secure Act 2.0, passed in 2022, helps those with student loans save for retirement by allowing employers to make matching contributions to employees' retirement plans, such as 401(k)s, based on employees' student loan payments. If you have student loans, it's worth researching whether your employer makes this match.[12]

I don't have enough money to invest. Many people believe they need a minimum of $1,000 to open a brokerage account (the account needed for buying and selling stocks and other securities), which is typically not the case. While some investment firms do require a minimum deposit, others have no minimum requirements. Nor do online trading platforms such as Robinhood and Webull.

I don't know how to open a brokerage account. Lack of knowledge about the mechanics of opening an account is no longer a valid reason to stay out of the market. There are numerous articles on the internet about how to set up an account—or you can simply go to Must-Know Fact 31 for instructions! Mobile trading platforms like Robinhood and Webull make things even easier—the apps walk you right through the setup process.

I want my funds to be in liquid assets. *Liquid* simply means that an asset can be converted to cash quickly. Different assets have different liquidity. Your savings and checking account are very liquid (they *are* cash). Your house is probably less so—that is, it takes longer to sell your house and get the cash from it. While it's wise to keep your regular bill-paying funds and emergency funds in a checking or savings account for safety and easy access, those types of accounts provide little return on your money. If inflation is 3% and you are earning 0.25% on your savings account, over time effectively you are *losing* 2.75% of your buying power. When you invest in stocks, mutual funds, ETFs, or similar securities, your money is held in assets that can grow your wealth for you—*and* they are relatively liquid. If needed (or when desired), you can typically sell these types of securities and have cash in hand within a few days.

Investing in the stock market is just a form of gambling. Buying a stock without first doing your homework is definitely risky. Too often, people buy stocks based on FOMO—fear of missing out. They hear a friend or a pundit on TV or online talk up a stock, and then buy it without doing their own research. But if you turn yourself into an educated investor, your investments will produce much better returns than a slot machine.

I don't know enough to invest in the market! According to Unbiased's *2023 Financial Confidence Survey*, 47 percent of Americans are uncomfortable making investment decisions.[13] And according to The Economist Group, even among investors, 61 percent express concern about their ability to make good investment decisions.[14] So if this is you, you're not alone. I think people with this problem are the smart ones: knowing what you don't know is important. But I'd like you to turn that statement into "I don't know enough to invest in the market—*yet*." This book will help you get started.

And if you are an unseasoned investor with limited time or desire to dig into investing details, there are many trustworthy financial advisors who make it their job to understand the market; they can provide you with customized financial guidance and help you make informed decisions. An advisor's annual fees generally run between 0.25% and 2% of the money they are managing on your behalf, which may be well worth it for their expertise and your peace of mind.

It's also worth noting that many people who invest in the stock market are not purchasing individual stocks directly. They are *indirect* stockholders—that is, they invest in mutual funds and exchange-traded funds (ETFs), often through financial vehicles like their employers' 401(k) plan or an IRA, as we discussed briefly above. Those are solid options too, and they take less effort than managing individual stocks.

Whatever your reasons have been in the past for not investing, if you've picked up this book, it's because you've made the decision to move beyond them. So let's get you the information you need to move from wannabe investor to *actual* investor!

ALLANISM

Buy only what you understand.

MUST-KNOW FACT 2
Stock is an ownership stake in a company.

*The individual investor should act consistently
as an investor and not as a speculator.*
BENJAMIN GRAHAM, AUTHOR OF *THE INTELLIGENT INVESTOR*

———————————
————————

A *stock* is a piece of a public company that you can own. If the company becomes more valuable, its stock price is likely to increase, earning you a return on your investment.

The words "stock" and "share" are often used interchangeably. Technically, *stock* refers to the ownership you have in a company, while *share* refers to each unit of ownership you buy. For example, you might have 10 shares of Apple stock, meaning 10 units of ownership of the company. Sometimes, you'll also hear people in the investment world use the term *equities*. Though that term can have some more complicated meanings, in most contexts it just means stocks—the tiny fractions of companies that investors own.

Broadly speaking, there are eight different types of stock, though not every company fits neatly into only one category. They are:

BLUE-CHIP STOCKS
Blue-chip stocks are from long-established companies that are leaders in their industries. They also are generally regarded as having the lowest investment risk because the companies' performance is usually stable

and fairly predictable. A few examples of blue-chip stocks are Procter & Gamble (PG), Microsoft (MSFT), and Berkshire Hathaway (BRK-B).

INCOME STOCKS

Income stocks regularly distribute some of their profits to their shareholders in the form of dividends. Dividends are typically paid quarterly and are usually deposited to shareholders' brokerage accounts in cash. However, some income stocks pay their investors in additional shares. Utility and energy companies such as Chevron (CVX), Verizon (VZ), and Progress Energy (PGN), among others, fall into this category.

GROWTH STOCKS

Growth stocks are from companies that have been expanding their sales, profits, or both at a rapid rate, and that are projected to grow rapidly for some time to come. But those expectations are not guarantees; besides having higher upside potential, these stocks also carry a higher level of risk. Often, in order to plow money back into supporting that rapid growth, executives choose to operate at a loss or with only modest profits for years. And not all growth companies manage to transition to solid profitability—hence the risk. Three that did successfully navigate that transition are Tesla (TSLA), Amazon (AMZN), and Nvidia (NVDA).

VALUE STOCKS

Value stocks appear to be undervalued in the market—that is, trading at a lower price than the company's reputation, earnings, outlook, or financial situation would seem to merit. Often, the reasons for being undervalued relate to short-term thinking in the market, so patient investors who buy these stocks can prosper over the long term. A few examples of stocks currently in this category are Disney (DIS), Lowe's (LOW), and the Ford Motor Company (F).

CYCLICAL STOCKS

When a company's performance is tightly linked with the broad health of the economy, its stock is considered a *cyclical stock*. At any given time, the US economy will be going through one of four stages: expansion, peak, contraction, or trough (the low point before recovery begins). Many cyclical stocks can reliably be expected to rise when the economy is in the first two stages and fall during the second two. Examples include car manufacturers, such as General Motors (GM); airlines, such as Delta (DAL); and hotel chains, such as Marriott (MAR).

Also in this category are companies whose health is tied to the supply-and-demand situation within their specific (and oscillating) market. Chip-makers, for example, have a pattern of building out their manufacturing capacity when supplies are tight, demand is strong, and their profits and stock prices are rising. This eventually leads to oversupply, plunging chip prices, and falling share prices. But inevitably, the cycle goes around again. So semiconductor leaders such as Intel (INTC) belong in this category, along with Nvidia (remember I said not every company fits neatly into only one category).

DEFENSIVE STOCKS

Defensive stocks come from well-established companies that are typically far less affected by the economic cycle than cyclical stocks are. Think Walmart (WMT), Coca-Cola (KO), and McDonald's (MCD). The average defensive stock also has a wide *economic moat*—a term coined by Warren Buffett to refer to a company's durable competitive advantages over its rivals and would-be rivals. (We'll talk more about economic moats in Must-Know Fact 16.)

Defensive stocks are considered to be more advantageous than other stocks in their sectors because they enjoy a consistent demand for their offerings, pay attractive dividends, and have stable business models. The downside is that they are much less likely to provide investors with explosive growth. (How many more McDonald's can the world handle, after all?)

SPECULATIVE STOCKS

Many younger companies have yet to prove that their business models will work, or that the products they hope to sell will actually perform as advertised, so their stocks are considered *speculative stocks*. Stocks in this category are particularly risky because they tend to move on rumors and hopes more than on solid business metrics. Speculative stocks may surge quickly, providing big gains for shareholders; however, they have the potential to drop just as fast, which can lead to substantial losses. While financial analysts offer opinions on many types of stock, they are less apt to cover speculative stocks due to the lack of company track records upon which to base educated opinions.

Stocks in this category include clinical-stage biotechnology companies such as Intellia Therapeutics (NTLA), which is developing gene therapies. Intellia will earn profits only if (probably someday far down the road) the treatments it develops prove effective and safe enough to earn regulatory approval. Similarly, QuantumScape (QS) is developing a new type of battery that could significantly speed up electric vehicle recharging, but until we see how well its tech works in the real world and whether it can be manufactured in a cost-effective way, there's no certainty about whether QuantumScape will deliver on its promise. Mining and exploration companies that are looking for new energy and mineral reserves are also considered speculative stocks.

PENNY STOCKS

Penny stocks, by definition, typically trade for less than $5 a share. Although a few penny stocks trade on the major US exchanges, most are sold over the counter (often abbreviated OTC), meaning through a broker-dealer network. The most common network is OTC Markets

Group Inc. In general, penny stocks are even more speculative—that is, riskier—than the stocks in the speculative category. Since they are usually young businesses, it can be hard to find reliable information about them, and companies traded over the counter are not subject to as much scrutiny from government regulators as companies traded on the exchanges. Additionally, because penny stocks normally trade at fairly low volumes, they are more subject to short-term manipulation. While these cheap stocks may have the potential for greater upside, they also carry the potential for deeper downsides.

ALLANISM

You get what you pay for.
Buy quality stocks!

———————

MUST-KNOW FACT 3

A stock exchange is a marketplace where stocks and other securities can be bought and sold. The stock market is the collection of those exchanges.

Having seen a non-market economy, I suddenly understood much better what I liked about a market economy.
ESTHER DYSON, FOUNDER OF WELLVILLE

———————

Stock exchanges have been around since the thirteenth century, when the merchants of Venice began trading government securities. The model upon which modern stock markets are built was born in the 1500s in Belgium with the Bourse at Antwerp—a commodities exchange where rights to physical goods as well as promissory notes were traded.

But the first true stock exchange was inaugurated about 150 kilometers north of Antwerp. If you're ever on *Jeopardy!* and the clue is "The first formal stock exchange still in existence today," press your buzzer and answer confidently, "What is the Amsterdam Stock Exchange?"

Today, there are sixty stock exchanges globally, and most list thousands of companies. However, according to Statista, as of July 2023, only nineteen of those exchanges have market capitalizations (the total value of all the companies they list) of more than $1 trillion USD, as shown in Table 1.

Table 1. Stock exchanges with market capitalization greater than $1 trillion

Exchange	Symbol	Market Cap
New York Stock Exchange	NYSE	$25.0 trillion
National Association of Securities Dealers Automated Quotations	NASDAQ	$22.2 trillion
Shanghai Stock Exchange (China)	SSE	$7.1 trillion
Euronext Amsterdam	AEX	$7.0 trillion
Japanese Exchange Group	JPX	$6.0 trillion
Shenzhen Stock Exchange (China)	SZSE	$4.8 trillion
Hong Kong Exchanges (China)	HKEX	$4.6 trillion
National Stock Exchange of India	NSE	$3.7 trillion
London Stock Exchange (U.K.)	LSE	$3.3 trillion
Toronto Stock Exchange (Canada)	TSX	$3.1 trillion
Saudi Stock Exchange	Tadawul	$3.0 trillion
Deutsche Boerse (Germany)	FSX	$2.2 trillion
Swiss Exchange	SIX	$2.0 trillion
Korea Exchange	KRX	$2.0 trillion
NASDAQ Nordic and Baltics	OMX	$1.9 trillion
Australian Securities Exchange	ASX	$1.7 trillion
Taiwan Stock Exchange	TAI	$1.7 trillion
Tehran Stock Exchange (Iran)	TSE	$1.6 trillion
Johannesburg Stock Exchange (South Africa)	JSE	$1.2 trillion

The US is home to the two largest exchanges: the New York Stock Exchange (NYSE) is the largest, and the NASDAQ (National Association of Securities Dealers Automated Quotations—the full name is rarely used) is the second largest. (If you are ever given the *Jeopardy!* clue "In 1971, this became the world's first electronically traded stock market," hit that buzzer and declare, "What is the NASDAQ?")

Being listed on a stock exchange offers several advantages to a company. It makes it simpler for the company to raise capital by selling new shares of stock. Public ownership distributes the financial risk across a larger group of stakeholders, including institutional and individual investors. And the company gains greater visibility by being discussed among analysts and investors.

Each stock exchange sets its own listing criteria, meaning that companies must meet certain requirements for their stocks to be listed on the exchange. Like private social clubs, stock exchanges set these requirements based on the reputation they want to preserve. For instance, the NYSE requires firms to have at minimum 1.1 million publicly traded shares with a collective market value of at least $40 million ($100 million for worldwide trading). The NASDAQ requires firms to have at least 1.25 million publicly traded shares with a collective market value of at least $45 million. Both require a minimum share price of $4 per share. Additionally, companies must meet one of four other sets of financial standards related to earnings, cash flow, capitalization, revenue, or assets and liquidity. The NASDAQ also looks for companies with a solid history and top-notch management to help maintain its well-respected position—a cachet it can share with the companies that list on it.

Here are three interesting facts that wannabe (and for that matter, seasoned) investors might not know about stock exchanges:

A stock can be listed and traded on multiple exchanges. One benefit of choosing to be listed on multiple exchanges is that it increases the shares' liquidity by making them easily accessible to more potential buyers and sellers. In addition to reaching a broader investor base, companies listed with more than one exchange offer investors more flexible trading time from exchanges located in multiple time zones. Multinational companies are often listed on several stock exchanges. For instance, British Petroleum (BP) is listed on the London Stock Exchange, the Frankfurt Stock Exchange, and the New York Stock Exchange.

Companies that stop meeting an exchange's criteria can be delisted. In addition to the requirements to join an exchange, there are requirements to *stay* on an exchange. If a company stops meeting the criteria, it can be *delisted*—removed from the stock exchange. For example, as mentioned earlier, both the NASDAQ and NYSE require a minimum stock price of $4 to be listed, but to stay listed, the price must remain above $1 a share. If the stock drops below $1 for more than thirty days, it runs the risk of being delisted.

There's no minimum size for a stock exchange. Launched in 2012, the Cambodia Securities Exchange (CSX) started with only one state-owned enterprise trading on its platform: the Phnom Penh Water Supply Authority (PPWSA). CSX added its second company in 2014, and it's still the smallest functioning stock exchange in the world, with only seven listed companies, two of which joined it in 2021. The second-smallest stock exchange is the Lao Securities Exchange (LSX), which currently includes only eleven companies.

ALLANISM

Rome wasn't built in a day.
Neither will be your success in the market.

_____

MUST-KNOW FACT 4
A bear market is when the market has lost 20 percent or more of its value from its recent peak and is trending downward.

The most important lessons in investing
are learned in the tough times.
HOWARD MARKS, OAKTREE CAPITAL MANAGEMENT

———————

Animals have a way of showing up in the strangest places. They even have an ongoing presence in the stock market! As you begin reading the financial news, you are certain to see bulls and bears mentioned. If your curiosity is piqued, as mine was, about how these animals came to be associated with the stock market, let me give you some background.

In the early eighteenth century, the phrase "bear market" emerged in connection with traders selling bearskins. Traders were known to make deals to sell bearskins at high prices—skins they didn't yet own. The traders were gambling that the going rate for bearskins would fall before they needed to deliver them, which would allow them to purchase the skins from trappers at a cheaper price and make a greater profit reselling them. Thus developed the proverb: "It is not wise to sell the bear's skin before one has caught the bear."[15] That is, ensure the value is there before making the deal.

In the twenty-first century, a *bear market* is a period of sustained declines in the values of stocks or other assets. According to the definition used by the US Securities and Exchange Commission (SEC), a bear market occurs when stock prices fall by 20 percent or more typically for two months or more. This trend is usually measured using a benchmark indicator such as the Standard & Poor's 500 index (S&P 500). Kadi Arula of the financial news site Finbold asserts that the term bear market comes from the sweeping downward motion of a bear's claw when it strikes—an apt metaphor for the painful downward sweep of a falling stock market.[16]

A bear market can be triggered by an economic decline or slowdown, consumer pessimism, negative investor sentiment—or a combination. While there's a pretty firm definition that allows you to say a bear market has *begun*, the question of determining when it *ends* can be a bit hazy. Historically in the United States, bear markets have lasted anywhere from a few months to a few years. The next bull market (see Must-Know Fact 5) following a bear won't begin until the market in question has risen by 20 percent or more. That means that there will be periods considered neither bulls nor bears.

For investors, the downward period of a bear market can be highly stressful, so let's put those plunges into historical context. As measured via the S&P 500, historical bear markets have lasted an average of close to nineteen months, with market value losses averaging around 38 percent. Take a look at Table 2, which shows the data for specific bear markets.

When we're in bear territory, a common question arises: will it become a recession? While a bear market is indicated by a market dip of 20 percent or more, the basic definition of a *recession* is a period in which the broader economy contracts in a deep and sustained way for at least two consecutive quarters (though the US government's definitional criteria are more complex).

**Table 2. Historical bear market declines as measured by the S&P 500
(Source: S&P 500 Indices)**

Start Date	End Date	Start Value	End Value	Length	Index Decline
Sep 7, 1929	Jun 1, 1932	31.92	4.40	32.8 months	86.2%
Mar 6, 1937	Apr 29, 1942	18.68	7.47	61.8 months	60.0%
May 29, 1946	Jun 14, 1949	19.25	13.55	36.5 months	29.6%
Aug 2, 1956	Oct 22, 1957	49.64	38.98	14.7 months	21.5%
Dec 12, 1961	Jun 27, 1962	72.64	52.32	6.5 months	28.0%
Feb 9, 1966	Oct 7, 1966	94.06	73.20	7.9 months	22.2%
Nov 29, 1968	May 26, 1970	108.37	69.29	17.8 months	36.1%
Jan 11, 1973	Oct 3, 1974	120.24	62.28	20.7 months	48.2%
Nov 28, 1980	Aug 12, 1982	140.52	102.42	20.4 months	27.1%
Aug 25, 1987	Dec 4, 1987	336.77	223.92	3.3 months	33.5%
Jul 16, 1990	Oct 11, 1990	368.95	295.46	2.9 months	19.9%
Mar 24, 2000	Oct 9, 2002	1,527.46	776.76	30.5 months	49.1%
Oct 9, 2007	Mar 9, 2009	1,565.15	676.53	17.0 months	56.8%
Feb 19, 2020	Mar 23, 2020	3,386.15	2,237.40	1.1 months	33.9%
Jan 3, 2022	Oct 10, 2022	4,796.56	3,583.07	9.2 months	25.3%
Averages		n/a	n/a	18.9 months	38.5%

According to David Zeiler, associate editor for *Money Morning*, a bear market is not necessarily a sure signal that a recession is coming.[17] In fact, four of the eleven bear markets between 1946 and 2009 had no corresponding recession. See Table 3 for the historical details.

When talking about declining markets, analysts use two other terms that you should know. A *market correction* is a period when the market has fallen by 10 percent to 20 percent from its fifty-two-week high. A *pullback* is a short-term drop in an asset's value, usually between 5 percent and 10 percent.

Table 3. Historical Bear Markets and Link to Recession (Source: LPL Research FactSet)

Month of Peak	Month of Low	Time to Trough	Recession?	Decline
May 1946	May 1947	12 months	No	29%
Aug 1956	Oct 1957	14 months	Yes	22%
Dec 1961	Jun 1962	6 months	No	28%
Feb 1966	Oct 1966	8 months	No	22%
Dec 1968	May 1970	17 months	Yes	36%
Jan 1973	Oct 1974	21 months	Yes	48%
Nov 1980	Aug 1982	21 months	Yes	27%
Aug 1987	Dec 1987	4 months	No	34%
Jul 1990	Oct 1990	3 months	Yes	20%
Mar 2000	Oct 2002	31 months	Yes	49%
Oct 2007	Mar 2009	17 months	Yes	56%
Apr 2011	Oct 2011	5 months	No	19%
Sep 2018	Dec 2018	3 months	No	20%
Feb 2020	Mar 2020	1 month	Yes	34%
Jan 2022	Oct 2022	10 months	No	25%

Navigating a bear market requires resilience, strategic decision-making, and a steadfast focus on long-term goals, but hang in there—you can get through those types of challenging market conditions.

ALLANISM

Stay calm when the stock market is volatile.

MUST-KNOW FACT 5
A bull market is when the market has gained 20 percent or more from its most recent low and is trending upward.

In a bull market, everyone becomes an expert!
In a bear market, everyone becomes wise!
AMIT TRIVEDI, INDIAN FILM SCORE COMPOSER,
MUSIC DIRECTOR, SINGER, AND LYRICIST

———————
————

Now that you know about bear markets, let me acquaint you with their opposite, *bull markets*.

The term bull market came into use after the term bear market did, as a way to differentiate the two swings in market conditions. Whereas a bear market describes a phase when stocks have *declined* by 20 percent or more from their recent high, a bull market describes a phase in which stock prices have *increased* by at least 20 percent from their previous low over at least a two-month period. A bull market is often indicated by the activity on the S&P 500 index, the Dow Jones Industrial Average (DJIA), or the NASDAQ Composite index.

One theory on why the bull was chosen to represent a rising stock market is the animal's movements: when a bull attacks, it charges and thrusts its horns *upward*. And, as already mentioned, when a bear attacks, it usually swipes its paw *downward*.

A bull market occurs when there is more demand to buy stocks than can readily be met by those who wish to sell them. The economy is usually strong, with solid economic growth (often measured by gross domestic product, or GDP); there is often a drop in unemployment and a rise in corporate profits. With optimism prevailing in the market, more initial public offerings (IPOs) may be issued.

There have been fourteen bull markets in the US since June 1932. Although analysts may try to project how long a bull market will last, it's really anyone's guess. As Table 4 shows, the shortest US bull market lasted just over twenty-one months, with the S&P 500 increasing 114 percent. The longest bull market occurred between 2009 and 2020 and lasted about 131 months, during which the index rose by 400 percent.

Table 4. Bull markets as measured by the S&P 500 (Source: S&P Dow Jones Indices)

Start Date	End Date	Start Price	End Price	Length in Months	Change
Jun 1, 1932	Mar 6, 1937	4.40	18.68	57.1	324.5%
Apr 29, 1942	May 29, 1946	7.47	19.25	49.0	157.7%
Jun 14, 1949	Aug 2, 1956	13.55	49.64	85.6	266.3%
Oct 22, 1957	Dec 12, 1961	38.98	72.64	49.7	86.4%
Jun 27, 1962	Feb 9, 1966	52.32	94.06	43.5	79.8%
Oct 7, 1966	Nov 29, 1968	73.20	108.37	25.8	48.0%
May 26, 1970	Jan 11, 1973	69.29	120.24	31.6	73.5%
Oct 3, 1974	Nov 28, 1980	62.28	140.52	73.9	125.6%
Aug 12, 1982	Aug 25, 1987	102.42	336.77	60.4	228.8%
Dec 4, 1987	Jul 16, 1990	223.92	368.95	31.4	64.8%
Oct 11, 1990	Mar 24, 2000	295.46	1,527.46	113.4	417.0%
Oct 9, 2002	Oct 9, 2007	776.76	1,565.15	60.0	101.5%
Mar 9, 2009	Feb 19, 2020	676.53	3,386.15	131.4	400.5%
Mar 23, 2020	Jan 3, 2022	2,237.40	4,796.56	21.4	114.4%
Averages				**59.6**	**177.8%**

Navigating a bull market requires a strategic blend of optimism and risk management, and a keen understanding of market dynamics. In such a dynamic financial landscape, as investors ride the wave of upward trends, staying vigilant, disciplined, and adaptable is essential for long-term success.

ALLANISM

Don't worry about timing the market; focus on your time *in* the market.

———————

MUST-KNOW FACT 6
Dividends are payments distributed by a public company to its shareholders from its earnings.

A cow for her milk, a hen for her eggs, and a stock, by heck,
for her dividends. An orchard for fruit, bees for their honey,
and stocks, besides, for their dividends.
JOHN BURR WILLIAMS, ECONOMIST

———————

Dividends can be a great way to expand your investing returns. If you understand how they work and how to best use them to your advantage, you can multiply the value of your portfolio faster.

Dividends are payments made to shareholders based on profits. More established companies tend to pay dividends. In fact, more than 84 percent of S&P 500 companies do. Just because a company pays a dividend, however, does not mean that it will always do so; sometimes dividends are suspended due to financial trouble or unexpected expenses a company is facing.

Companies pay dividends for three main reasons. First, regularly giving shareholders a percentage of a company's profits incentivizes people to buy its stock, and to value it more highly, resulting in a higher share price. Second, dividends can encourage shareholder retention. And finally, dividends demonstrate that the company's leaders are confident regarding its future.

Warren Buffett is famously happy to *collect* dividends—a majority of companies in the Berkshire Hathaway investment portfolio pay them. But his remarkably successful conglomerate has never *distributed* dividends. Why?

There are three main reasons profitable companies may choose *not* to pay dividends. First, some companies prefer to reinvest their profits into attempting to grow their businesses. Second, some may be conserving cash for future acquisitions. And finally, some may need to use their cash to pay down debt.

Companies still in their early, relatively rapid growth stages rarely pay dividends. Many of these companies are not yet profitable, and they are focused on acquisitions, expansion, revenue growth, product development, research and development, and other things that require all the capital they can muster.

Dividend Payments

The vast majority of US companies that distribute dividend payments do so quarterly, but a tiny fraction of them (just fifty-eight, at last count) pay their dividends monthly.

Some companies pay out dividends in cash; some pay out dividends as additional shares of stock; and some give an option of shares or cash.

When a stock in your portfolio pays a cash dividend, you typically have a choice of two options:
1. Receive the payout as cash.
2. Reinvest your cash dividends into more shares of that company's stock.

With either option, dividends are considered taxable income, so you are responsible for paying taxes on your dividend income for the tax year in which you receive it. The tax rate depends on whether they are *ordinary dividends*, which are taxed at your usual marginal income rate, or *qualified dividends*, which are taxed at (typically lower) capital gains rates. To be considered qualified, dividends must meet certain IRS criteria, including a minimum holding period. (We will talk about capital gains tax rates in Must-Know Fact 37.)

If the company makes dividend payments in shares only and there is no cash option, you typically do not pay taxes on the dividends received until the shares are sold. However, if you are given a cash option, the dividends are taxable, even if taken as shares.[18]

If the dividend-paying stock is held in a tax-deferred account such as a 401(k) or an IRA, or an education savings plan such as a 529 Plan or Coverdell Education Savings Account (ESA), you do not owe taxes until that stock is sold.[19] Please note, however, that tax-deferred accounts have a number of rules and caveats that we can't cover here, so do your research before investing in them.

It's important to understand the tax implications of your investments, including the impact of dividends and tax-deferred plans, so be sure to consult with a tax professional to get advice specific to your situation.

ALLANISM

Play the long game.

––––––––––

MUST-KNOW FACT 7
A dividend reinvestment plan (DRIP) uses the proceeds generated from dividend stocks to automatically purchase more shares of the company.

*Most investors want to do today
what they should have done yesterday.*
LARRY SUMMERS, FORMER US SECRETARY OF THE TREASURY

———————

In the prior section, you learned about two options for cash dividends: taking them as cash or reinvesting them to purchase more shares of that company's stock. Some people prefer cash dividends to use as a source of income. Others choose to reinvest their dividends and increase the number of shares they hold, to continue taking advantage of increases in the stock price.

To take your dividends in cash or reinvest them: That is the question!

To know which is better for you, let's look at some possible scenarios, but first, some quick terminology . . .

The *record date* is the day when a company locks in the list of shareholders to whom it will pay dividends on the next *payout date*. The *ex-dividend date*, which is the day before the record date, is the date after which a stock is traded without an investor having the right to the next dividend. The eligibility for shareholders to receive the next dividend is based on having bought the stock *before* the ex-dividend date. Investors who own a stock a minimum of at least two days before the record date and hold the shares until the ex-dividend date are eligible for the next dividend.[20]

Now back to our scenarios . . .

Let's say you bought 10 shares of Broadcom (AVGO) at the end of trading on April 8, 2022, when it closed at $592.54 per share. On June 21 (the ex-dividend date), you still own those shares and are entitled to the $4.10 per share dividend the company will pay out on June 30, so $41 total.

Should you take that $41 in cash, or reinvest it in shares? Let's look at both options.

Cash option: If you choose to receive dividends as quarterly checks, you can use the $41 however you want. And if you own an assortment of other dividend-paying stocks, your quarterly checks could start to really stack up. Over time, some investors even live off dividend yields.[21]

Reinvestment option: If you choose to reinvest that $41 dividend, you will receive approximately 0.08 shares of AVGO. While a fraction of a share may not seem like much, reinvesting your dividends repeatedly can make a *huge* difference over ten, twenty, or fifty years.

Asset manager Joshua Kennon wrote an article that beautifully illustrates this point.[22] Kennon asks us to imagine a couple of identical investors who each invested $10,000 in Coca-Cola (KO), a dividend-paying stock, and held on to it for fifty years.

Now, Kennon starts his clock in 1962, but I don't want to simply borrow his work and calculations, so I'm going to run my own numbers, using a different (though overlapping) time period. Our twin investors, Jason and Jennifer, made their investments on January 2, 1974. During that day's session (conveniently for our math), Coca-Cola shares traded at around $125, so their $10,000 investments bought them 80 shares each.

Here's where our twins' paths diverged: Jason opted to receive the cash every quarter, while Jennifer chose to reinvest all her dividends.

From 1974 through January 2, 2024, Jason collected a total of $213,750 in cash from his dividends. Moreover, in the course of those fifty years, thanks to Coca-Cola's six stock splits, his original 80 shares grew into 7,680 shares with a market value of about $460,000. Not bad!

Like Jason, Jennifer began with 80 shares. However, because she reinvested her dividends into buying more shares, during that same fifty-year period, her stake in Coca-Cola grew to more than 18,900 shares with a market value of about $1,132,000! And that is the power of compound growth (which we'll discuss further in the next Must-Know Fact).

In this example, for the sake of simplicity, I haven't discussed the impact of taxes and potential commissions, but I recommend you consult your tax professional for guidance.

There are legitimate reasons to take dividends in cash, income being one of them, but if you have fifty, twenty, or even ten years, consider reinvesting your dividends so that compound growth can work for you.

ALLANISM

**Let the power of compounding work
for you by reinvesting your dividends.**

MUST-KNOW FACT 8

Compound growth is one of the most powerful tools for increasing your invested wealth.

The compound effect is the principle of reaping huge rewards from a series of small, but smart choices.
DARREN HARDY, AUTHOR OF *THE COMPOUND EFFECT*

―――――――
―――――――

If you aren't familiar with the Groner Foundation, you should be—not just because it is a fine nonprofit that promotes service-learning opportunities for college students, but because in the life of its founder, Grace Groner, we find an amazing example of the power of compound growth.

Groner began working at Abbott Laboratories in 1931, soon after she graduated college. In 1935, she bought 3 shares of Abbott (ABT) stock at a price of $60 a share. (Note: Her $180 investment in 1935 was equal to about $4,044 in inflation-adjusted 2023 dollars.) She never actively bought another share, but simply left her investment alone and allowed it to grow. When she died in 2010 at age 100, that $180 had grown into a stake of more than 100,000 Abbott shares worth $7.2 million![23]

Groner's 3 shares of stock grew to 100,000 shares partly because Abbott split its stock repeatedly. As we'll discuss later, stock splits increase the number of shares an investor has in a company.

However, even if Abbott stock had never split, the value of Groner's $180 initial investment would still have grown to $7.2 million thanks to the combination of dividend reinvestment and the power of compound growth.

If you've ever had a savings account, you are probably familiar with compound growth, in the form of compound interest. *Compounding* is simply the ability of money to grow exponentially over time by the repeated addition of earnings to the principal.[24] In your savings account you earn interest each month. That interest is added to the principal, and the following month, interest is calculated based on the new sum. As the principal increases, the earnings increase in proportion. Unfortunately, most savings accounts today offer low rates of interest, so their ability to compound your money isn't as strong as that of the average stock portfolio, especially if you reinvest your dividends.

The concept of compounding might be easiest to understand by example:

- You invest $1,000 in a stock. In year one, the stock provides a return (i.e., growth) of 10%, or $100, so your investment's value at the end of that year is $1,100.
- In year two, the stock has the same return of 10%; however, this time your gain is $110, because the earnings are based on $1,100 (rather than on just the original $1,000), so now you have $1,210.
- In year three, that same 10% return gives you a gain of $121, for a year-end value of $1,331.

Every year, you benefit from new growth on the old growth—and the accelerating growth continues.

The not-so-secret ingredient for making the most of the power of compound growth is time. The earlier you begin to consistently invest in the stock market, the greater the benefits you can reap from the power of compounding.

You may be saying to yourself: "I don't have decades for compound growth to work before I retire!" You might not have fifty years—nor are you likely to be setting your cash aside untouched for seventy-five years as Groner did—but I bet you have at least ten or twenty.

I've created a chart (Table 5) to show you how investing $100 a month (a mere $3.33 a day) will grow thanks to that magic word: *compounding*. But while our 10% return rate makes the arithmetic easy, it might sound overly optimistic, so let's be conservative: what is a realistic rate to expect from the stock market over time?

Dr. Jeremy Siegel is the Russell E. Palmer Emeritus Professor of Finance at the Wharton School of the University of Pennsylvania and the author of the award-winning book *Stocks for the Long Run*, now in its sixth edition. (I consider his book a must-have for your investing library.) Siegel examined the US markets over the extremely long term and found that between 1802 and 2021, the total real returns of US indexes—*after* accounting for the declining value of the dollar due to inflation—averaged out to a compound annualized return of 6.9%.

To be even *more* conservative, in my chart, I used a compound annual return of 6%. Take a look now at Table 5 to see what you can accumulate by investing just $1,200 a year, at a rate of $100 a month, if your portfolio grows at a compound annualized rate of 6%.

In year one, if you invest $100 each month over the course of twelve months and get a 6% compound annualized return, your money will grow to $1,234 by year end. (You might be wondering why your 6% gain on $1,200 isn't $72. It's because you didn't put the whole $1,200 in at the start of the year.) As you go deeper into the chart, you'll see how the value of that portfolio you've added to consistently grows exponentially. That happens because of one simple principle: *compounding*!

In ten years, your $12,000 in contributions grows to $16,388, an increase of more than 36%. However, the longer you give the power of compounding to work, the more profitable your strategy becomes. During the subsequent decade, as you add another $12,000, for an invested total of $24,000, the value of your portfolio grows to $46,204—a return on investment of more than 92%! And remember, we picked a growth rate that takes inflation into account. That's a near doubling of the *real value* of your money. So what are you waiting for? Begin your investing plan today!

Table 5. The power of compound growth ($100 a month, 6% annualized rate)

Year	Total Contributions	End-of-Year Portfolio Value
1	$1,200	$1,234
2	$2,400	$2,543
3	$3,600	$3,934
4	$4,800	$5,410
5	$6,000	$6,977
6	$7,200	$8,641
7	$8,400	$10,407
8	$9,600	$12,283
9	$10,800	$14,274
10	$12,000	$16,388
11	$13,200	$18,632
12	$14,400	$21,015
13	$15,600	$23,545
14	$16,800	$26,230
15	$18,000	$29,082
16	$19,200	$32,109
17	$20,400	$35,323
18	$21,600	$38,735
19	$22,800	$42,358
20	$24,000	$46,204

ALLANISM

No matter your time horizon, put the power of compound growth to work as soon as possible.

———

MUST-KNOW FACT 9
Identifying your risk tolerance is an essential factor for your investing success.

In a world that is changing really quickly, the only strategy that is guaranteed to fail is not taking risks.
MARK ZUCKERBERG, FOUNDER OF FACEBOOK

———————
————

In investing, *risk tolerance* is simply your ability and willingness to stomach big declines in the value of your investments. Your risk tolerance is a personal decision, and it probably won't stay the same throughout your whole life. It's impacted by your age, your financial situation at any given time, and your investment goals. But even more, your risk tolerance reflects your personality. High-risk people can ride the investment rollercoaster without losing their nerve; low-risk folks want more of an even keel. There's nothing wrong with either preference, but recognizing your level of risk tolerance is vital, because making investment choices that suit that level will allow you to sleep better at night.

Levels of Risk Tolerance

Read the following descriptions of typical high-, medium-, and low-risk-tolerant investors to assess your level of risk tolerance. You might even circle the bullets that sound like you to see which category fits you best.

This type of assessment (and there are plenty such tools online) will be instrumental in determining the type of financial vehicle that is best suited for you.

LOW RISK TOLERANCE

If you are a low-risk investor, you tend to:

- Want to minimize the possibility of financial loss of your investments.
- Prefer the preservation of capital over potential returns.
- Feel uneasy about market volatility and significant fluctuations in the value of your investments.
- Need access to funds sooner to pay for upcoming college expenses or retirement funding.

Therefore, as a low-risk investor you should opt for safer, more conservative investment options such as bonds or stable, dividend-paying stocks.

MEDIUM RISK TOLERANCE

If you are a medium-risk investor, you tend to:

- Want a balance of risk and potential return.
- Accept a moderate level of market fluctuation.
- Feel more comfortable diversifying your portfolio with a mix of stocks and other assets.
- Prioritize a certain level of stability balanced with growth and a measured amount of risk in your investment strategy.
- Have a longer time horizon before you'll need to withdraw your money and have other liquid assets available.

As a result, you will likely want to consider stocks, including those from varied sectors and industries, but not overly speculative or highly volatile ones. Diversifying with some bonds and more conservative assets in the mix may also be advisable.

HIGH RISK TOLERANCE

If you are a high-risk investor, you tend to:

- Be more adventurous, and comfortable with the potential for significant market fluctuations.
- Be willing to take on substantial risk in pursuit of higher returns.
- Take a long-term perspective and understand that the value of your investments can experience notable ups and downs.
- Embrace a more aggressive approach, accepting the possibility of substantial losses in exchange for the potential for higher rewards.

As a result, you can consider investing in more volatile stocks, emerging markets, or innovative sectors.

I hope that gives you some idea of your risk tolerance. You may not fit neatly into just one category, though—and you don't have to.

Sample Investors with Varying Risk Tolerance

Let's now look at a few scenarios and discuss how individuals with low, medium, and high risk tolerances might make investment choices. And if you're not quite sure where you fall yet, see how you respond to their respective situations.

SCENARIO 1: LOW-RISK-TOLERANCE TERRY

Terry is a single forty-five-year-old woman who works as a computer programmer. Each year, she contributes enough to her 401(k) to max out her employer's matching contributions, and she has an emergency fund large enough to cover her living expenses for one year. She is thrifty and has saved $20,000, which she has kept in a high-yield savings account so that her cash will be liquid. Between 2010 and 2023, that savings account paid an annual interest rate of 3.75% and grew her $20,000 to $32,540—a total return of 62.7%.

Recognizing that she has a low tolerance for risk, Terry is comfortable with the tepid growth of her initial investment. What she has not taken into account is inflation, which averaged approximately 2.75% during that time, resulting in her investments increasing her purchasing power by just 1%. And if the interest Terry was earning had been, say, 2.5%, *below* the rate of inflation, she would have been *losing* buying power.

For conservative investors in particular, it's important to understand your *nominal* gains (the absolute dollar amount) versus your *real* gains (gains in buying power). While investing conservatively doesn't mean you *can't* keep up with inflation, if you keep your money in a savings account, you may find yourself losing money when you factor inflation into the equation.

SCENARIO 2: MEDIUM-RISK-TOLERANCE TOM

Tom was thirty-two when he got his first taste of investing. On January 1, 2010, his birthday, he received 351 shares of Coca-Cola, valued at slightly more than $20,000, from his grandmother. Her request was that Tom hold this value stock until he turned forty-five on January 1, 2023.

When he received the shares in 2010, Coca-Cola stock was priced at $57 per share. By January 3, 2023, the stock was valued at $62.95 a share—but it had also split 2-for-1 once in the intervening years. As a result of this split, he now owned 702 shares, with a total value of $44,191. This amount doesn't include the dividends Tom received over the years, which added up to $12,369. Had he reinvested those dividends, his stake would have been worth $56,559 when he turned forty-five.

SCENARIO 3: HIGH-RISK-TOLERANCE TINA

Tina was a forty-year-old entrepreneur and small business owner. She had about $30,000 to invest and decided to go for broke by putting it all into growth stocks.

On January 4, 2010, she invested in a trio of businesses that looked like they had the potential for exponential growth: eHealth, an online service that helped people sort through the health insurance market to find policies suitable for them; Cleveland BioLabs, a clinical-stage biotech company that was working on some promising treatments; and Repligen, a company that developed drugs as well as manufactured materials for use by other drugmakers. That day, Cleveland BioLabs closed at $70 a share, eHealth closed at $17.12, and Repligen closed at $3.79. For $10,010, Tina bought 143 shares of Cleveland BioLabs. For $9,998, she purchased 584 shares of eHealth. And for $9,998 more, she purchased 2,638 shares of Repligen.

Her plan was to hold those stock positions for at least fifteen years. That long-term approach is right in principle, but it doesn't always work. When it does, be assured that the stock price fluctuations are not for the weak of heart, particularly if you're investing in companies before they've truly proven themselves.

Online-focused eHealth stagnated for a few years before surging in late 2013, rising to a cyclical peak above $60 in January 2014—more than tripling her investment. But just as fast as it had risen, it fell. One year later, her investment was in the red, and it stayed there for years. Then, in 2018, the business began to rise again—this time it was even more pronounced. By spring 2020, even as the pandemic was taking hold, the stock was above $130, approaching a 700% return! Then it began to tumble and oscillate again, with a whole lot of sharp moves, both up and down. But the downtrend dominated, and though Tina held on hoping for a comeback, on January 3, 2023, eHealth closed at a mere $4.85 a share. Her $9,998 had dwindled to $2,832.

With Cleveland BioLabs, she fared even worse. In the first two years of her investment, Tina watched the shares rise above $150; after that, they sank steadily. By mid-2012, her investment was in the red, and the slide continued. The day before the company vanished in a merger, its stock price was a mere $3.17. Less than $500 remained of her original investment.

But what about Repligen? Turns out that manufacturing the materials needed to produce biologic drugs was a good business to be in, as more and more of those types of treatments were developed. Though the stock has slumped from the $300-plus peak it hit in September 2021, Tina has little reason to be unhappy. On January 3, 2023, Repligen stock closed at $162 a share, making her stake worth $427,356.

The moral of the story: High risk does not always result in high reward. If your stomach can't tolerate the wild rides of an eHealth or the disappointment of a Cleveland BioLabs, aim to pick less aggressive stocks—because nobody can be sure that the aggressive growth stock they are picking will turn out to be a Repligen.

Now that you have read about three people with three different risk tolerance levels, which one do you most identify with:

- Low-Risk-Tolerance Terry, who preferred safety over risk and saw her $20,000 savings account balance grow by a total of 62.7% over a thirteen-year period to $32,540?
- Medium-Risk-Tolerance Tom, who was a middle-of-the-road investor and saw his $20,000 invested in Coca-Cola stock more than double in value over thirteen years (and would have tripled if he'd reinvested his dividends)?
- High-Risk-Tolerance Tina, who bought somewhat speculative growth stocks with approximately $30,000 in 2010 and saw her money grow by more than 1,300% over a thirteen-year period, even though two of her picks cratered?

Understanding and acknowledging your risk tolerance is paramount for any new stock market investor and allows you to lay a solid foundation for your financial journey. Whether you lean toward a conservative-, medium-, or high-risk approach, aligning your investment strategy with your risk tolerance helps manage expectations and mitigates the emotional stress associated with market fluctuations. It ensures that your hard-earned money is invested in a manner that aligns with your financial goals and psychological comfort, fostering a more sustainable and prosperous investment experience over the long term. As financial markets inherently involve uncertainties, the clarity you gain by identifying and respecting your risk tolerance is critical to building a resilient and personalized investment strategy.

If you are still unsure how much risk you can tolerate, schedule time to talk with a financial professional who may be able to guide you. They can help you assess your risk tolerance and create an investment plan tailored to your individual needs.

ALLANISM

Your risk tolerance may change based on your age, financial situation, and investment goals.

MUST-KNOW FACT 10
Asset allocation is the "pie chart" of investments in a portfolio.

I think the first thing is you should have
a strategic asset allocation mix that assumes
that you don't know what the future is going to hold.
RAY DALIO, INVESTOR AND HEDGE FUND MANAGER

———————
————

In Must-Know Fact 9 we touched on the different types of investments someone with high, medium, or low risk tolerance might consider: stocks versus bonds versus savings accounts or CDs. In addition to having a preference for different types of assets, the *allocation* of different types of assets should vary depending on your risk tolerance and goals. The mix of different types of investments in your portfolio is called your *asset allocation*. Savvy investors often begin with the end in mind by developing their target asset allocation before even deciding in which financial vehicles they are going to invest.

Sample Portfolio Allocations

Thinking about the risk levels we just discussed, let's look at some fairly typical portfolio allocations for low-, medium-, and high-risk investors.

THE CONSERVATIVE APPROACH

Someone who has a lower risk tolerance and/or needs access to funds soon might choose to invest 50% in bonds, 30% in short-term investments (such as CDs, money market accounts, and high-yield savings accounts), 15% in US stocks, and 5% in foreign stocks. See Figure 1. Annual returns will likely be lower than those in a more aggressive portfolio, but there will also be less volatility.

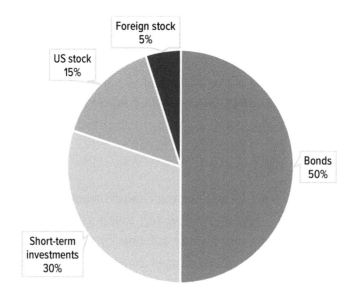

Figure 1. Sample conservative portfolio allocation

THE MODERATE APPROACH

Our medium-risk investor, who is willing to be more aggressive than our conservative investor, might choose an allocation such as 30% in bonds, 15% in short-term investments, 40% in US stocks, and 15% in foreign stocks. See Figure 2. While the average annualized return might be higher when taking a moderate approach compared to a conservative one, this investment mix will have more market volatility. If you have committed to investing in the market long term, there is a good chance you will experience market fluctuations. When you do, remember, "when there is no risk, there is no reward."

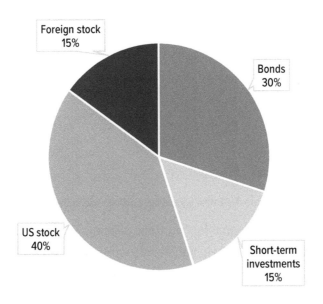

Figure 2. Sample moderate portfolio allocation

THE AGGRESSIVE APPROACH

If you're the kind of person who lives by the saying, "You have to risk failure to experience success," then an aggressive growth asset allocation may be your cup of tea—or rather, strong espresso! High-risk-tolerant investors might consider an allocation of 60% to US stocks, 25% to foreign stocks, and 15% to bonds. (Notice no short-term investments.) See Figure 3. There will almost certainly be more volatility in this portfolio than in the prior two, but if you think long term, you've got the potential for a higher payoff!

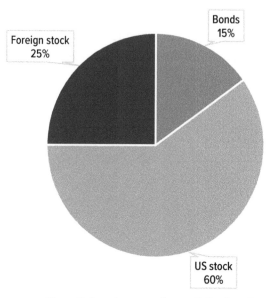

Figure 3. Sample aggressive portfolio allocation

If you go online and search for "portfolio allocation models," you'll find several models that may help you decide which asset allocation is right for you. Some models may have four, five, or even eight different suggested asset allocations based on your goals and risk tolerance. (Now do you see why I hammered on risk tolerance so hard?)

Portfolio Rebalancing

After you decide on a targeted asset allocation for your portfolio and invest in assets that meet your needs, periodically review how your allocation percentages change. There's a good chance your investments will grow at different rates, eventually changing the proportions of the investments in your portfolio. For example, if your initial asset allocation was 50% stocks and 50% bonds and, over time, your stocks increased in value while the value of your bonds remained stagnant, your asset allocation could theoretically change to 70% stocks and 30% bonds.

If you are wondering how to stay aligned with your 50/50 asset allocation, you use a process called *rebalancing your portfolio*. Portfolio rebalancing allows you to reallocate your assets to either your initial percentage mix or to one that better fits your current financial needs. It's always good to keep an eye on your investment mix, but at least once a year assess whether it's time to rebalance. And of course, keep in mind that you will never be *precisely* at your 50/50 goal—the idea is to be materially close so that you maintain the degree of risk you intended to.

ALLANISM

Choose investments based on your risk tolerance, research, and time horizon.

———————

MUST-KNOW FACT 11
Stock market crashes might be painful; however, they don't last forever.

If you aren't thinking about owning a stock for ten years,
don't even think about owning it for ten minutes.
WARREN BUFFET, CO-FOUNDER OF BERKSHIRE HATHAWAY

———————
————

As we've already established, investing in stocks is one of the best ways for you to grow your money in the long term. As Allan emphasized to me many times before I began investing, the key phrase is "long term." Patience is definitely a virtue when it comes to investing in the stock market. There will be times when the entire US market falls by as much as 30 to 50 percent—you read that right—and your portfolio balance may fall that much or even more!

Investors who are not emotionally prepared for these types of drops often react by panicking and selling some or even all of the stocks in their portfolio. This locks in their loss rather than allowing the investments to regain value. But remember: what goes down will also go up when the market recovers. After you review the data describing the last five recessions, you will see that maintaining a logical mindset rather than panic selling pays off.

I want you to have the knowledge to understand what is happening and make decisions from a place of information and logic, not from a place of fear that you will lose your hard-earned money. So read on to learn about several selloffs from the past few decades, how long it took the stock market to recover, and, best of all, the financial reward you would have earned by remaining logical and staying in the market. To calculate the projections I've included, I used NerdWallet's Stock Market Crash Calculator. Although this tool is no longer available, you can find similar calculators by searching online.

THE DOUBLE-DIP RECESSION (1980–1982)

In the early 1980s, a number of factors collided—oil prices, inflation, high interest rates, US monetary policy, and high unemployment—leading to a recession.

Your $100,000 portfolio would have dropped to $71,700 at the bottom of the cycle but recovered in about two years. And if you'd hung on to it until December 31, 2019, the value would have reached $2,299,160.

BLACK MONDAY (1987)

Attributed to global geopolitics and the introduction of computerized trading (which accelerated matters), the October 19, 1987, crash is known for being the largest single-day decline in US stock market history—about 22 percent. The market recovered within two years.

If you had $100,000 in your portfolio at the time, on Black Monday the value would have dropped to $79,200. However, it would have recovered from the loss in approximately two years. And your portfolio value as of December 31, 2019, would have reached $1,142,830.

DOT-COM BUBBLE (2000)

During the 1990s, internet-related ventures were the hot thing. The market got overheated and the tech bubble burst in 2000. The S&P 500 dropped about 50 percent and took about seven years to recover.

If you had $100,000 in your portfolio when the dot-com bubble began to burst in March 2000, your portfolio's value at the bottom would have been $50,800. However, if you had remained calm and held on to your investments, your portfolio would have recovered and returned to its original value of $100,000 in seven years and two months, and it would have grown to $211,500 by December 31, 2019.

THE GREAT RECESSION (2007–2009)

The Great Recession of 2007–2009 was a result of the 2000s housing bubble and subsequent subprime mortgage crisis. The S&P 500 lost about half its value and took about two years to recover.

If you had $100,000 in your portfolio at the start of the Great Recession, your portfolio's value at the bottom of the sell-off would have been $43,200. That's a steep drop. However, if you had avoided joining the panic-selling group, your portfolio would have returned to its October 2007 peak value of $100,000 in five years and five months. And your patience would have been rewarded over the longer term. Your portfolio's value would have reached $206,400 by December 31, 2019, giving you a compound annual growth rate of about 6.2% across that whole span. And remember, that would be your gain even if you had put all your money into the market at the worst possible time—right before the crash.

COVID-19 (2020)

And of course, our most recent recession came due to the COVID-19 pandemic. In March 2020, the Dow fell nearly 13 percent in one day. After the federal government stepped in to support the economy, the market began to rise, and by August it had recovered.

One thing is certain in investing: when you put your money into the stock market for the long term, you are bound to experience stock market crashes. The impacts of those crashes on your finances will be based in part on the level of risk you have built into your portfolio and in part on how you respond to the crash.

I hope you can see why I say repeatedly that you should be prepared to hold your investments where they are for at least ten years. There will be ups and downs, but pulling your money out too quickly will cost you the gains you would accrue by being patient and fully participating in the rebounds that have always followed major drops (so far, at least in the US market).

No matter when it happens, a stock market crash is unnerving. One way to make a stock market crash more palatable—if that is possible—is by diversifying your portfolio holdings. That's what we'll talk about next.

ALLANISM

Patience is a virtue, and that certainly applies when investing in the stock market.

———————

MUST-KNOW FACT 12

Diversification reduces your risk by spreading your money across a variety of asset classes and business sectors.

The most significant benefit of a diversified portfolio is the psychological stability when you need it the most.

NAVED ABDALI, AUTHOR OF

INVESTING: HOPES, HYPES, & HEARTBREAKS

————————
————

Before we talk about the many investment options available to you, let me share the most concise piece of investing wisdom that Allan ever imparted to me: *Diversify*!

Why Diversify Your Portfolio

Diversifying your portfolio means spreading your investments across different asset classes, sectors, and individual stocks. Doing this minimizes the impact of any single investment's performance—good or bad—on your portfolio.

For example, contrast the widely diversified portfolio of Warren Buffett's Berkshire Hathaway—which holds banks and beverage companies, automakers and consumer goods sellers, tech leaders, and energy giants (and more)—with the highly focused approach of Ark

Invest founder and CEO Cathie Wood, whose exchange-traded funds (ETFs) contain only tech sector companies and related ambitious innovators. If you had money in the Ark Innovation ETF in 2020, you would have felt like a genius as you watched it more than triple while Berkshire Hathaway lagged. And even in 2021, you probably wouldn't have minded much as it dipped a bit and went sideways—your bet on just a few hot sectors would have still had you running well ahead of those who opted for broad diversification.

But in 2022, your lack of diversification would have clobbered you. Tech and growth stocks crashed that year, and value stocks came back into vogue. Compared to Ark Innovation's much wider ups and downs, from January 2020 through September 2023, the steady performance of well-diversified Berkshire Hathaway left the tech ETF in the dust.

The benefits of diversification apply to conservative and aggressive investors alike.

- **Reduced risk:** By diversifying your portfolio, you minimize the impact of any single investment on your portfolio. This means you are less likely to suffer a significant loss if one investment performs poorly.
- **Steadier returns:** By spreading your investments across different asset classes, sectors, and individual stocks, you may achieve more consistent returns over time.
- **Lower volatility:** A diversified portfolio may experience lower volatility than a concentrated portfolio, which can help investors stay the course during market downturns.
- **Increased flexibility:** A diversified portfolio allows investors to more easily adjust their investments as market conditions change.

Diversification is an essential principle of investing, and it's a necessity when investing in the stock market so that you protect the money you worked so hard to earn.

How to Diversify Your Portfolio

With all that in mind, here are five common ways to diversify your portfolio:

Invest in a variety of asset classes. Spread your money across US stocks, foreign stocks, bonds, and short-term investments like CDs, money market accounts, and high-yield savings accounts.

Invest in several of the eleven stock business sectors. Spread your investments across several of the eleven business sectors, such as technology, healthcare, finance, and energy. (We'll talk about the sectors in Must-Know Fact 14.)

Invest in different types of stocks. Spread your investments across large-cap, mid-cap, and small-cap stocks. (We'll talk about market capitalization and why it matters in the next Must-Know Fact.)

Invest internationally. Stock exchanges in other countries list the public companies in those nations. And, as noted earlier, some foreign companies also trade on US exchanges. Because foreign companies are enmeshed in their local economies (as opposed to the US economy), they experience different business conditions than US companies do. To profit from the growth potential of those other economies, invest in companies in different countries and regions.

Use exchange-traded funds and index funds. We'll go into greater detail about exchange-traded funds and index funds in Must-Know Facts 20 and 21, but for now, let's sum them up this way: these investment vehicles hold large portfolios of stocks or bonds, and allow you to gain easy diversification with a single investment.

ALLANISM

Diversify!

——————
——————

MUST-KNOW FACT 13
Market capitalization reflects the total value of a company's outstanding shares.

Price is what you pay. Value is what you get.

WARREN BUFFETT, CO-FOUNDER OF BERKSHIRE HATHAWAY

———————

As you start reading about the stock market, here are some terms you'll likely encounter:

- Nano-cap stocks
- Micro-cap stocks
- Small-cap stocks
- Mid-cap stocks
- Large-cap stocks
- Mega-cap stocks

"Cap" is short for capitalization. A company's *market capitalization* (or market cap) is the total market value of all the outstanding shares (shares available for purchase) of a company. It is calculated by multiplying the number of outstanding shares by the current price per share.

Let me give you an example: If a publicly traded corporation has 15 million shares outstanding, and it currently trades at $20 per share, it would have a market capitalization of $300 million. Therefore, as you'll learn below, that particular company would be considered a "small-cap."

NANO-CAP STOCKS

Nano-cap stocks are publicly traded companies with market caps under $50 million. As of August 2023, according to the website Stock Analysis, there were 971 companies in this category on the US market. These are usually penny stocks (with share prices below $5), typically traded over the counter rather than on the larger exchanges.

MICRO-CAP STOCKS

Micro-cap stocks have market capitalizations between $50 million and $300 million. In June 2022, the folks at NASDAQ said that there were about 4,300 exchange-listed micro-cap public companies, and another 2,700 being traded in the over-the-counter market. Both micro-cap and nano-cap stocks can be highly risky investments, for a number of reasons. Due to their small size and their (usually) relatively brief tenures as publicly traded entities, there will be limited information about them available to investors. Professional analysts generally don't cover them. They trade less often, so, in Wall Street jargon, they have "lower liquidity"; that is, when you want to sell shares, you may find it harder to complete those trades. And finally, such thinly traded and low-priced stocks are more subject to being manipulated by people attempting to game the market. This is not to say that you should never buy nano- or micro-cap stocks, but do your research carefully, and remember: buyer beware.

SMALL-CAP STOCKS

Small-cap stocks are companies with market capitalization between $300 million and $2 billion. In December 2012, there were around 1,989 companies in this category (the number changes frequently and the definition sometimes varies). A few names you may recognize:
- Shutterstock (SSTK), with a $1.6 billion market cap.
- La-Z-Boy (LZB), with a $1.4 billion market cap.
- Warby Parker (WRBY), with a $1.7 billion market cap.

While I originally thought that stocks in this category were younger, more speculative organizations, that's not always the case. And though small-caps may be riskier investments than mid-caps and large-caps, they can also have greater capacity for growth—it's a whole lot easier for a company to make big improvements to its sales and earnings from a small base than from a large one. Because of this, as a class, small-caps can at times outperform large-caps. Moreover, even companies within the small-cap category are often well-established organizations.

MID-CAP STOCKS

Mid-cap stocks have market caps between $2 billion and $10 billion. There are around 1,100 companies in this category. Three names you may recognize:

- Yelp (YELP), with a $3 billion market cap.
- Hasbro (HAS), with a $9.1 billion market cap.
- Whirlpool (WHR), with a $7.8 billion market cap.

Mid-cap stocks are generally less volatile than small-cap stocks, and both small-cap and mid-cap stocks tend to be less affected by global situations—think the trade war between the US and China and its resulting tariffs—than large-cap stocks are. In addition, since mid-caps are established businesses, they usually can secure financing when they need or desire it more easily than small-caps can.

LARGE-CAP STOCKS

Large-cap stocks have market caps of $10 billion to $200 billion. As of December 2023, there are about 735 companies in this category. Here are three brands you are bound to know:

- Starbucks (SBUX), with a $122 billion market cap.
- Netflix (NFLX), with a $140 billion market cap.
- CVS Health (CVS), with a $120 billion market cap.

These stocks tend to be more stable because these are typically mature companies. Stocks in the category tend to be less volatile, with company revenue and earnings growth typically steady and stable. Companies that are not in high-growth mode pour fewer resources into stimulating growth, so they are more likely to pay consistent dividends to shareholders instead. And when it comes to well-established, long-public large-cap companies, there's usually plenty of reliable research data available.

MEGA-CAP STOCKS

Mega-cap stocks have market caps of $200 billion or greater. As of August 2023, there were forty-two of them. These are by far the largest publicly traded companies. Three that fall within this category are:

- Apple (AAPL), with a market cap of $2.8 trillion.
- Microsoft (MSFT), with a market cap of $2.6 trillion.
- Amazon (AMZN), with a market cap of $1.4 trillion.

Which type of company is better? Well, unsurprisingly, each has its advantages and disadvantages. But here I must share one key piece of advice that investing guru Allan shared with me: "Don't get too hung up on a company's market cap. An organization's market cap does not always tell an investor how much the business is worth. Its market cap simply demonstrates how valuable the public perceives it to be."

My conclusion: Not everything is as clear-cut as we'd like it to be, including market capitalization!

ALLANISM

Don't get hung up on a company's market cap.

———————

MUST-KNOW FACT 14
The eleven stock business sectors provide a framework for organizing and analyzing companies based on their primary business activities.

One of the very nice things about investing in the stock market is that you learn about all different aspects of the economy. It's your window into a very large world.
RON CHERNOW, BIOGRAPHER, JOURNALIST, AND HISTORIAN

————————

The corporate world can be divided into eleven business sectors, and understanding them can help you see and interpret the market's natural ebbs and flows. The most widely used system for sorting companies today is the Global Industry Classification Standard (GICS), which was jointly developed by Morgan Stanley Capital International and the S&P Dow Jones Indices in 1999. Their purpose was to place each company into the category that most accurately represented its operations, and thus assist analysts, investors, and others in comparing like with like. In other words, GICS groups similar companies together and gives us one more analytical tool to use in making investment decisions.

As of early 2023, the number of domestic and international stocks listed on the two main US exchanges alone totaled 5,996, with 2,385 companies on the NYSE and 3,611 on the NASDAQ.[25] That's a lot to sort through, so every tool can help. Let's look at each of the sectors.

SECTOR 1: ENERGY

This group is composed of companies that deal with oil, gas, coal, and other consumable fuels. A few familiar companies in this sector are:

- Marathon Oil (NYSE: MRO)
- Chevron (NYSE: CVX)
- ExxonMobil (NYSE: XOM)
- Halliburton (NYSE: HAL)
- ConocoPhillips (NYSE: COP)

SECTOR 2: MATERIALS

This group includes companies that deal in all manner of materials, such as metals, concrete, wood and paper products, and chemicals. A few familiar companies in this sector are:

- United States Steel (NYSE: X)
- Linde (NYSE: LIN)
- BHP Group (NYSE: BHP)
- Rio Tinto (NYSE: RIO)
- Vale (NYSE: VALE)

In a *Forbes* article, financial writer David Rodeck explains that while these stocks may lose value during economic downturns, they tend to rise in value when there is more demand for houses, cars, electronics, and other products. He also says they tend to pay higher average dividends than the other sectors.[26]

SECTOR 3: INDUSTRIALS

This sector is composed of a broad array of businesses, including construction, engineering, electrical equipment, logistics, and more. It includes companies focused on capital goods, aerospace and defense, transportation and logistics, and construction and building supplies. A few familiar companies are:

- United Parcel Service (NYSE: UPS)

- RTX (NYSE: RTX)
- Union Pacific (NYSE: UNP)
- Honeywell (NASDAQ: HON)
- Caterpillar (NYSE: CAT)

SECTOR 4: CONSUMER DISCRETIONARY

This group is composed of companies that produce and sell things like cars, consumer electronics, clothing, household items, and luxury goods, but also service providers like hotels, restaurants, and movie theaters. A few familiar companies in this sector are:

- Amazon (NASDAQ: AMZN)
- Tesla (NASDAQ: TSLA)
- Home Depot (NYSE: HD)
- Toyota (NYSE: TM)
- Nike (NYSE: NIKE)

You might be surprised to find Amazon in this category, even though you probably buy things from it often. While it can also be viewed as a technology company (and its technology businesses are where it makes the lion's share of its profits), the experts behind the GICS have concluded that the best description for it is Consumer Discretionary.

SECTOR 5: CONSUMER STAPLES

These companies sell frequently purchased items, such as food, beverages, tobacco, non-durable household goods, and personal products—things that, unlike those in the discretionary category above, people have a lot more trouble doing without. A few companies in this sector are:

- Procter & Gamble (NYSE: PG)
- PepsiCo (NASDAQ: PEP)
- Estée Lauder (NYSE: EL)
- Unilever (NYSE: UL)
- Philip Morris International (NYSE: PM)

Consumer staples companies are generally less sensitive to economic cycles because even when people's budgets are tight, they still spend on what they view as necessities.

SECTOR 6: HEALTH CARE

This sector includes drug manufacturers, companies that build medical devices, pharmacy benefit managers, and healthcare providers. Some companies in this sector are:

- Vertex Pharmaceuticals (NASDAQ: VRTX)
- Align Technology (NASDAQ: ALGN)
- UnitedHealth Group (NYSE: UNH)
- HCA Healthcare (NYSE: HCA)
- AMN Healthcare Services (NYSE: AMN)

SECTOR 7: FINANCIALS

This sector includes banks, insurance companies, brokerage houses, consumer finance providers, and mortgage real estate investment trusts. Some investors—among them, Warren Buffett—like to invest in financial sector companies because they can accumulate and generate enormous amounts of cash. Some companies in this sector are:

- Atlanticus Holdings (NASDAQ: ATLC)
- B. Riley Financial (NASDAQ: RILY)
- Blackstone (NYSE: BX)
- CorVel (NASDAQ: CRVL)
- KKR & Co. (NYSE: KKR)

SECTOR 8: INFORMATION TECHNOLOGY

This is the sector for businesses that create hardware and software. Some prominent companies in this sector are:

- Apple (NASDAQ: AAPL)
- Microsoft (NASDAQ: MSFT)

- Taiwan Semiconductor Manufacturing (NASDAQ: TSM)
- Nvidia (NASDAQ: NVDA)
- Broadcom (NASDAQ: AVGO)

SECTOR 9: COMMUNICATION SERVICES

These companies provide services such as broadband networks, mobile wireless networks, and television broadcast networks. Some familiar names in this sector are:

- T-Mobile (NASDAQ: TMUS)
- Comcast (NASDAQ: CMCSA)
- Netflix (NASDAQ: NFLX)
- Meta Platforms (NASDAQ: FB)
- Alphabet (NASDAQ: GOOGL, GOOG)

SECTOR 10: UTILITIES

The companies in this sector supply core infrastructure needs, such as electricity, natural gas service, and water. A few companies you might recognize in this sector are:

- NextEra Energy (NYSE: NEE)
- American Water Works (NYSE: AWK)
- Dominion Energy (NYSE: D)
- Duke Energy (NYSE: DUK)
- Brookfield Infrastructure Partners (NYSE: BIP)

Investors often see the stocks in this sector as great long-term holdings for dividend income and stability. They are viewed as solid picks during economic downturns, as demand for these services tends to remain stable.

SECTOR 11: REAL ESTATE

These companies own, develop, lease, and manage properties and land. Some stocks in this sector are:

- CBRE Group (NYSE: CBRE)

- Simon Property Group (NYSE: SPG)
- Prologis (NYSE: PLD)
- American Tower (NYSE: AMT)
- Equinix (NASDAQ: EQIX)

Some companies change sectors. Comcast and Netflix, for instance, used to be part of the Consumer Discretionary, and Meta (formerly Facebook) and Alphabet (formerly Google) were originally part of the Information Technology sector. However, in September 2018 when GICS updated its classification criteria and the Telecommunication Services sector was renamed the Communication Services sector, Comcast, Netflix, Facebook, and Google were shifted into it.[27]

Knowing and understanding these business sectors gives you a leg up on diversifying your portfolio. The more knowledge you have, the better investment decisions you can make!

ALLANISM

Do your research rather than making an impulsive purchase.

————

MUST-KNOW FACT 15
A stock split does not change the value of an investor's holdings; it simply changes the number of shares.

This is one of the keys to successful investing:
Focus on the companies, not on the stocks.
PETER LYNCH, INVESTOR AND AUTHOR

———————
———————

You will find a few perks when investing in the stock market. One may be the remarkable discovery that the number of shares of a particular stock in your portfolio has doubled, tripled, quadrupled, or even increased by a factor of twenty overnight.

You read that right: Sometimes, the number of shares you own in a company can increase without your having to do anything. Can you guess how that could happen? If you think it's some kind of "stock share bonus day," sadly, there is no such thing. Neither is there a fairy godmother of investments who goes around slipping shares under your pillow. Admittedly, one could picture a dividend reinvestment plan as something like a quarterly stock share bonus day. Once you set it up, you don't have to think about it again, but—surprise—every three months like clockwork, the number of shares you own will grow. But that growth is small and gradual. What I'm talking about here is something completely different. It's something we've already mentioned, but now it's time to look at it in depth: stock splits.

How a Stock Split Works

When you see the number of shares of a stock in your portfolio multiply literally overnight, you are witnessing a *stock split*. This describes a publicly traded company's action to increase the number of shares held by existing investors by splitting them, thus bringing down the per-share price and making more shares available.

Let me give you an example: It is common for companies whose shares have increased significantly in value to do a 2-for-1 stock split. If you owned 50 shares of that company's stock on the *record date*, the cut-off date by which you and other shareholders must own shares of that stock to receive a split, you would be eligible to have twice the number of shares issued to you. After the split, you would have 100 shares of that stock in your portfolio.

Keep in mind, however, that while you have twice the number of shares, the total value of those shares will be (more or less) the same. When a stock splits 2-for-1, the price of each individual share is sliced in half. Imagine a blueberry pie. Whether you cut that pie into four, six, or eight pieces, the amount of pie on the plate remains the same. The same principle applies when a company splits its stock.

Here is a quiz that will help you understand how a stock split works:

> **Question 1:** If you bought 10 shares of Apple stock in July 2020 and on August 28, 2020, Apple split its shares 4-for-1 (which it did, by the way), how many shares of Apple would you own on August 29?
> **Answer:** If you said 40 shares, you are right!

> **Question 2:** Following that 4-for-1 stock split, how much would each share be valued at?
> **Answer:** Did you say that each share would have been

worth one quarter of its price before the 4-for-1 split? If you did, then you are right once again! While your 10 shares increased by a factor of four, the dollar value of each stock also decreased by a factor of four, because that one stock split into 4 shares. Imagine taking a slice of that blueberry pie and slicing it further into four slivers. The portion on your plate remains the same.

Question 3: How would the record date impact your stock's eligibility for the split?

Answer: If you said, "They would have been eligible for the 4-for-1 split only if I owned the 10 shares of Apple on the record date," I would commend you and say you are in luck: Apple's record date was August 24, 2020. Since you owned your 10 shares of Apple a month before its August 24, 2020, record date, you would have been eligible for the 4-for-1 split!

Many new investors wonder if buying a stock after it splits is more advantageous than buying before the split occurs. The answer is that it doesn't matter. It's purely a psychological choice. Think about it for yourself: Would you prefer to buy 1 share of Nvidia at $700 before it split or 4 shares at $175 a share? As you probably concluded, you would be investing $700 either way. The timing of your purchase relative to the split has no impact on how much money you invest. However, some investors feel better buying more shares, so they would prefer to own 4 shares of stock at $175 each rather than 1 share at $700.

The Advantages of a Stock Split

Believe it or not, even though it does nothing to fundamentally change the value of the underlying company, a stock split does change how that stock trades. But don't take my "wannabe investor" word for it. That's the educated opinion of Phil Mackintosh, chief economist and senior vice president of NASDAQ.

According to a 2020 article by Mackintosh,[28] stocks that have split tend to outperform the market. In fact, he finds, just announcing an upcoming split causes those stocks to beat the market by 2.5% on average. Not only do lower-priced stocks often look more appealing to investors, stocks after a split turn out to be more "tradeable"—the inherent costs of buying and selling them are lower—and their liquidity increases. All of that pushes their values a bit higher. Stock splits also serve as an indicator of management's confidence that the company (and the stock) will continue to perform well.

If you are curious which companies have split their shares, you can find plenty of historical data at www.stockanalysis.com. It lists splits by year, and it allows you to sort by split proportions—2-for-1, 3-for-1, 4-for-1, 1-for-5, 10-for-1, and even 96-for-1!

Reverse Stock Splits

The 1-for-5 stock split listed above was *not* a typo. A stock split in which you end up with fewer shares than you held before is called a *reverse stock split*, and while in some ways it resembles a regular split—but backwards—the circumstances involved are usually quite different.

A 1-for-5 split means that shareholders will get 1 share of stock for every 5 shares they hold—with the new shares worth five times as much as the old ones. It's like taking those individual pieces of pie and fusing them into one big slice.

Why would a company perform a reverse split? Well, unfortunately, it rarely signals anything good about the state of the actual business. You'll recall that companies tend to perform standard stock splits after their share prices have risen significantly. Those businesses are thriving—

so much so that an average retail investor (like you and me) who might want to buy shares would find it hard to pick up more than a handful of them or, in some cases, even a single share.

In the case of a reverse split, shares have fallen so significantly that they have reached levels that could put many investors off for being too low—sometimes even into the penny stock range. Even more troubling, as you will recall from the earlier section on stock exchanges, a stock that falls below a certain level for a set period may be delisted—removed from trading on the exchange. By undergoing a reverse split, companies entering the danger zone can often avoid that fate.

Reverse splits can also serve to improve a company's image and visibility, but like a regular split, a reverse stock split has no real effect on a company's value. The market capitalization remains essentially the same after a reverse split is executed, so if the company does not accompany that maneuver with real changes to improve its business, the conditions that led to its falling share price may persist.

Let me give you a specific example of a company that underwent a reverse stock split. I owned General Electric (GE) stock in July 2021. On Friday, July 30, 2021, at the close of the trading session, GE performed a 1-for-8 reverse split. The reverse-split-adjusted shares were effective on the next trading day, Monday, August 2, 2021.

When the market closed on July 30, 2021, each share of GE stock was worth around $15.

Pop quiz! Let's see if you're clear on how the reverse split affected my holdings of GE stock:

> **Question 1:** If I owned 240 shares of GE on July 30, 2021, and this stock did a 1-for-8 reverse split, how many shares would I have owned on August 2, 2021?
> **Answer:** After the reverse split took effect, my 240 shares of GE stock became 30 shares.

Question 2: After the reverse split, what was the value of each share of GE stock?

Answer: $120 a share. The original 8 shares were worth $15 each. Then GE did the 1-for-8 split. To determine the new stock share value, simply multiply GE's pre-split share price of $15 by 8.

Whew. I bet you've had enough of stock splits. Keeping track of them is almost as challenging as doing a physical split!

ALLANISM

Avoid following a stock's daily price.

MUST-KNOW FACT 16

An economic moat is any durable advantage a company has that protects it from rivals and allows it to maintain long-term profitability and market share.

A business that makes nothing but money is a poor business.
HENRY FORD, FOUNDER OF FORD MOTOR COMPANY

———————
————

The great Warren Buffett first popularized the concept of the *economic moat*. The earliest public description of it came in 1993, when he was a guest speaker at a Columbia University investment class. Bruce Greenwald, the professor, asked Buffett how an investor could understand a company well enough to invest in it.

Buffett explained that he would not invest in a company unless it had a strong competitive advantage, what he called a "moat," that allowed it to hang on to its market share and maintain its profit margins, rather than have them be eroded by rivals. If you imagine a moat, you might think of a water-filled ditch surrounding a castle or fort to ward off attacks. Likewise, a company's moat is something that helps it defend itself from "attacks" by other companies.

Buffett has delivered many words of wisdom that any wannabe investor can learn from, but this concept is pretty important: he has often said that moats are among the main factors an investor should look for when choosing long-term investments.

Identifying Moats

Any number of competitive traits can help a company develop an economic moat, but there are some common ones. The six questions below can help you determine if a company you are interested in has some of those beneficial traits.[29]

1. Does the company have a *cost advantage*? When a company can sell its products or services at lower prices than its competitors, it is said to have a *cost advantage*. Walmart is an excellent example: it does an immense volume of sales, which allows it to negotiate lower prices with its suppliers; that, in turn, allows it to price its offerings for customers at levels that are hard for most of its competitors to replicate.

2. Does the company have a *network advantage*? A *network advantage* is when each additional user of a product or service makes it more useful and valuable. For example, consider social media platforms like Facebook, X (formerly known as Twitter), and Instagram. The greater the number of family and friends who use a platform, the more useful it is to you as a tool for keeping in touch with them. And when you join a social media network, the more appealing it becomes to people who are close to you. Someone might sing the praises of a newer platform like Mastodon, but with far fewer users, that platform's network effect is weaker, so you would probably be less likely to want to switch to it.

3. Are there *switching costs* to move from this company to a rival? When it takes significant time, effort, and/or money to change from one company to another, that's known as a *switching cost*. Switching costs are why many people stay with their bank, cable company, or cellular provider—it's a hassle to change, there are fees involved, and so on and so forth. But it's not just individual consumers who have to deal with switching costs: large companies, for example, are slow to change service providers and suppliers, because doing so can mean accepting a host of added short-term expenses and disruptions.

4. Does the organization have *brand recognition*? My favorite way to define and gauge *brand recognition* is when a consumer can correctly identify a particular product based on its service logo, tagline, or packaging. The golden arches of McDonald's, for instance, are recognizable by virtually everyone around the globe. A rival might make a great hamburger, but the brand power of McDonald's (not to mention its enormous scale) keeps customers coming through its doors.

5. Is there a *high barrier to entry*? If a new company wanted to build a competing operation, how costly, complicated, or time-intensive would it be to do so? The harder it is, the higher the *barrier to entry* is said to be. Consider cell phone providers like AT&T or T-Mobile. To even begin to offer a network with a similar level of wireless coverage would involve many years of construction and hundreds of billions of dollars in expenses. At this point, the big telecoms don't need to worry much about any new rivals pushing into their turf—the barriers to entry are simply too high.

6. Does the company have *intangible assets*? *Tangible assets* are things like buildings and equipment. *Intangible assets* include brands, franchises, patents, licenses, and intellectual property. Disney is a perfect example of a company with a strong moat of intangible assets. Any filmmaker can make a superhero movie or an adventure series on alien worlds, but only Disney can make a Marvel movie or a *Star Wars* series.

You may wonder if a company needs all six characteristics to be considered as having a moat. Not according to Pat Dorsey, who was the director of equity research for the investing giant Morningstar. In his 2008 book, *The Little Book That Builds Wealth: The Knockout Formula for Finding Great Investments,* Dorsey explained that in his view, there are four types of moats that provide the largest sustainable advantages: cost advantages, network effects, switching costs, and intangible assets. Each one is valuable, but a company doesn't need to have all of them.

Now let me put you to work to determine if the five companies below have moats, based on one or more of the above characteristics. If you decide that the company has one of the above characteristics, there is a good chance that it has a *narrow moat*. On the other hand, if you find that it has several of the above characteristics, it most likely has a *wide moat*. The wider the moat, the more stable the company should be.

Think about the companies, and then look at the answers that follow. On your mark, get set, moat! I mean, *go!*

1. Walmart
2. Amazon
3. Apple
4. Disney
5. Berkshire Hathaway

[Cue *Jeopardy!* theme song.]

And now, the answers:

1. Walmart (WMT): We started with a softball: Does the Arkansas-based giant have a moat? It sure does—and a wide one at that. As noted above, and as you are likely to have experienced personally, Walmart maintains a low-cost advantage over its competitors. Additionally, the company boasts 10,500 stores and clubs under forty-six banners in nineteen countries, and a massive e-commerce operation.[30] Even more interesting than that, 90 percent of all Americans live within ten miles of one of its stores. While Costco and Target may have a considerable edge over Walmart in customer satisfaction,[31] Walmart's lower prices and proximity to its customers keep people returning to it.

2. Amazon (AMZN): If you said that Amazon has a moat, you are right! Amazon has many competitive advantages: it has enormous scale all around, its retail platform makes shopping easy and *fast*, its cloud services have a huge barrier to entry, and its logistics have a network effect. And according to some analysts, it is still undervalued and has excellent growth potential.[32]

3. Apple (AAPL): If you said that Apple has a moat, you are right. Apple boasts one of the most valuable brand names in the world, which constitutes a powerful moat. Apple also has strong brand recognition and intangible assets with its iCloud services.[33]

4. Disney (DIS): Although the pandemic dealt a harsh blow to Disney's theme parks, stores, resorts, and cruise line, in addition to the intangibles we identified earlier, it has a market barrier that competitors cannot pierce. In fact, Mickey, Minnie, and their pals have earned a place in Morningstar's Wide-Moat Focus Index, which specifically tracks—you guessed it—companies with wide moats. Even better, as global investment management firm VanEck noted, Disney stock was one of the top five contributors to the Wide-Moat Index's growth in January 2023.[34]

5. Berkshire Hathaway (BRK-A, BRK-B): This might have been a trickier company to analyze since it is not a business-to-consumer company the way the first four are. So if you said yes it has a moat, bingo! Berkshire Hathaway has numerous competitive advantages: it has a known, respected leader (Warren Buffet); when it acquires a company, it hangs on to the talented management team; it has a long-term focus (which should not surprise you after the number of times I've mentioned Buffet's investment advice); and it has plenty of cash on hand and no debt. Additionally, this conglomerate has numerous individual subsidiaries with wide moats of their own.[35]

Moats Are Not Permanent

You might be wondering if companies can lose their moats. Sure they can!

Readers of a certain age will remember the internet behemoth AOL. In its heyday, it benefited from serious network effects. For a time, it felt like *everyone* was on AOL, so everyone *needed* to be on AOL. It was where the action was. But tastes change, technology changes, and eventually, its vast user base moved on. Goodbye, network effect. Goodbye, moat.

Others will recall Research In Motion (RIM), maker of the BlackBerry—one of the first widely adopted smartphones in the mid-2000s. RIM enjoyed incredible brand power, plus intangible assets in the form of its patented technology and network. No doubt many investors—and Black-Berry users—would have viewed its moat as formidable. They could never have guessed how quickly BlackBerrys would become obsolete after the iPhone debuted. Once Apple managed to overcome the high barrier to entry involved in creating a better smartphone—and the App Store ecosystem that underlay its appeal—it was all but over for RIM.

Economic moats provide protection for companies, just as physical moats did for castles. But invaders have captured castles for centuries, so think carefully as you assess just how secure those business moats really are. That will go a long way toward helping you make better long-term investment decisions.

ALLANISM

Rather than chasing stocks, choose solid investments and keep them for the long term.

————————

MUST-KNOW FACT 17

Safe investment vehicles generally offer lower returns than riskier investment options, but a higher level of security when it comes to capital preservation.

How many millionaires do you know who have invested in a savings account? I rest my case.
ROBERT G. ALLEN, AUTHOR OF *CREATING WEALTH*

———————

In Must-Know Fact 2, we talked about *value* and *growth*, two of the most important concepts to grasp when you start investing in the stock market. While stocks can be volatile, they also have a higher rate of return than virtually any other investment option. However, if you are a conservative investor or are thinking of diversifying your portfolio, this Must-Know Fact will familiarize you with several of the safer financial vehicles and summarize the advantages and disadvantages of each.

Most of these (except savings accounts) are forms of *fixed-income securities*—that is, they are investments that provide a known return through fixed periodic interest payments and the eventual return of principal at maturity. Compare that to stocks, for instance, where the return can fluctuate vastly and of course can even be negative. You can see the appeal of knowing your principal is safe and earning a return.

Fixed-income securities are *debt instruments*, with bonds being the most common form (we'll address bonds more specifically in Must-Know Fact 18). You essentially lend an entity (a business, a government, etc.) money in return for periodic interest payments and eventually the return of the principal. With fixed-income securities, the risk of losing the capital you've invested is minimal, and you can fairly accurately predict how much you will receive in interest. These investment options are particularly suitable for investors who are looking for a steady income stream, capital preservation, and lower volatility than stocks.

These are the types of investments I had my money in until I felt knowledgeable and confident enough to invest in stocks.

Savings Accounts

Chances are, you're quite familiar with savings accounts already, and for almost anyone likely to be reading this book, they offer a perfectly safe place to store money you don't intend to spend immediately but want easily accessible. *Savings accounts* are deposit accounts that are federally insured for up to $250,000 per depositor per insured bank per ownership category (e.g., single accounts, joint accounts), so even if your bank goes bust like Signature or Silicon Valley did in spring 2023, you'll still get at least that much of your money back. Savings accounts pay interest, but even the best accounts don't pay particularly high rates, so the growth you'll get from a savings account will rarely, if ever, keep up with inflation. If you're planning to keep a significant (for you) amount of cash in one, it's worth shopping around.

Advantages of savings accounts:
- Easy access to funds
- No lock-in period
- Liquidity
- Protection
- Low start-up cost

Disadvantages of savings accounts:
- Minimum balance requirements to avoid fees
- Federal withdrawal limits
- Low interest rates
- Rates can change

Money Market Accounts

A *money market account* is similar to a savings account in that it is an interest-paying account at a bank or credit union and is FDIC insured. It typically pays higher rates than a savings account, but the minimum deposit is often higher, and there may be fees associated with it. Similar to a checking account, a money market account may have check writing privileges, but the number of transactions allowed is usually limited (e.g., a few per month). However, if you have cash on hand that you don't intend to spend immediately but might want sometime soon, a money market account may be a better option than a savings account. But shop around!

Advantages of money market accounts:
- Higher interest rates than savings accounts (usually)
- Check writing privileges (or debit card)
- FDIC insured

Disadvantages of money market accounts:
- Higher minimum deposit requirements
- Limited number of transactions allowed
- Fees

Certificates of Deposit (CDs)

A *certificate of deposit* (CD) is a savings product in which you deposit a lump sum of money for a set period, during which you earn interest on that amount. At the end of the term, you get your principal back along with the interest. You can choose to take the cash, or you can reinvest it. CDs are typically purchased through banks or credit unions, or through a brokerage account. Unlike bank savings or checking accounts, they do not have monthly maintenance fees, but there may be a minimum investment required.

CD terms are commonly one, three, or five years, but can be as short as three months or as long as ten years. Note that you lose access to your money during that time—that is, it becomes *illiquid*—unless you pay a penalty (though you may find some exceptions). CDs typically have fixed rates, so when you purchase one, you know exactly what you'll be paid in interest, and exactly the date that the CD will mature. While fixed rate is the norm, you might see some variable-rate CDs as well. The longer the term, the higher the interest rate you receive. However, the risk of inflation sapping the value of your returns is just as real for CDs as it is for savings accounts. If the return on investment for the CD doesn't at least keep up with the rate of inflation while you're holding it, it will result in the loss of purchasing power over the long term.

One method people use with CDs is called *laddering*. This means dividing the amount of money you want to deposit into multiple CDs with different maturity dates. When each CD reaches its maturity date, you have a grace period to decide if you want to renew this "time deposit" or collect the cash. This strategy allows you to have some flexibility in accessing portions of your money over time and it mitigates *interest rate risk*—that is, the potential for rising interest rates to reduce the relative value of your investment—that you would face if all your CDs had the same maturity date.

A word of caution: If you buy CDs, be sure that the financial institution you're buying them through is an FDIC-insured bank or credit union. That way, your CDs will be insured up to a maximum of $250,000. If you are investing more than $250,000 in CDs, it's prudent to do so through more than one FDIC-insured institution to ensure that each investment is fully protected.

Advantages of CDs:
- Safety
- Guaranteed returns
- Higher returns than savings accounts
- Ability to ladder your CDs
- No monthly fees

Disadvantages of CDs:
- Lack of accessibility
- Early-withdrawal penalties
- Lower returns than stocks (in the long run)

US Treasuries

US Treasuries—Treasury bills, notes, and bonds—are widely considered among the safest assets in the world. Political posturing in Washington notwithstanding, the US federal government is almost certainly not going to default on its debts.

TREASURY BILLS

A *Treasury bill,* or T-bill, is any US debt obligation issued with a maturity date of one year or less (sometimes as little as a few months). In other words, they are short-term debt securities. A buyer purchases a Treasury bill for less than its face value—for instance, paying $97 for a $100 T-bill. At the end of the maturity period, the bill can be redeemed from the government for its face value. That $3 increase is the return. However, if the holder sells a T-bill before its maturity date, they could make or lose money, depending on the prices at which T-bills are trading at that time.

Interest on T-bills is taxed at the federal level, but not at the state or local level. So if you live in a state with a higher income tax rate, such as New York or California, T-bills can save you some money relative to other taxable investments.

Advantages of Treasury bills:
- Safety
- Liquidity
- Low minimum investment
- Competitive yields
- Tax advantages

Disadvantages of Treasury bills:
- Low returns (relatively)
- Inflation risk
- Risk of loss if sold before maturity

TREASURY NOTES AND TREASURY BONDS

Treasury notes, also called T-notes, have maturity terms of two, three, five, seven, or ten years. *Treasury bonds* have twenty-year or thirty-year maturities. In addition to their longer maturities, what makes both T-notes and T-bonds different from Treasury bills is that they pay out interest to their holders every six months until their maturity date, and they can be redeemed at any time, making them liquid. They also pay higher interest rates than T-bills; the longer you're "locking up" your money, the better the rate you can expect. We'll talk more about bonds in the next Must-Know Fact.

Advantages of Treasury notes and bonds:
- Government-backed
- Federal guarantee virtually eliminates default risk
- Liquid

Disadvantage of Treasury notes and bonds:
- Relatively low yields

ALLANISM

If there is no risk, there is no reward.

———————

MUST-KNOW FACT 18
Bonds are debt instruments that make periodic interest payments to bondholders until their maturity date, at which point the principal is repaid.

What I put in the stock market, I don't have to touch
for a lifetime. I want to live off my bonds.
I want to be that safe.
MONICA SELES, TENNIS CHAMPION

———————

We began talking about debt instruments, including bonds, in the prior Must-Know Fact. Now let's delve deeper into bonds.

The entity offering the bond is called the *issuer*. The issuer could be a government agency, a municipality, or a private entity, such as a corporation. The buyer, whether an individual or an institution, is sometimes referred to as the *holder*. The bond is essentially an IOU from the issuer to the holder, as the holder lends the issuer the money that has been invested. Each bond has a specific date when it is meant to be cashed in, which is termed the *maturity date*. That's when the holder gets the money (the principal) back. Between the date a bond is issued and its maturity date, interest is paid (just as you would pay interest on a loan from a bank). Those regularly scheduled distributions are called *coupon payments*.

Some bonds may be redeemed, or *called*, by their issuers at specific prices on one or more pre-determined dates before the maturity date—

these are termed *call dates*. If a bond is called, the bond issuer pays investors the call price (usually the face value of the bonds) along with interest accrued to date. At that point, the issuer stops making interest payments on the bond. An issuing company might choose to call its bonds if it is able to take out new debt at better terms; essentially, it uses the call dates as a mechanism to pay off its older, higher-interest debt and refinance at a lower rate. You may have done something similar if you ever refinanced your mortgage at a lower rate.

While bonds have lower risk levels than stocks, they still carry some risk. Paul Conley, an expert in investing and bonds, says that while bonds are generally considered safe investments, that safety varies based on the type of bond you purchase and the risk level associated with that bond.

Types of Bonds

The most common types of bonds include the following:

GOVERNMENT BONDS

Government bonds are issued by national governments, such as US Treasury bonds. Government bonds are considered the safest type because they are backed by the full faith and credit of the issuing government, and as a rule, stable nations don't want to default on their debts. That said, less stable countries have defaulted when their fiscal situations became untenable. Venezuela, for example, has defaulted several times in the modern era.

MUNICIPAL BONDS

Municipal bonds are issued by state or local governments to fund public projects, such as infrastructure construction. As an incentive for residents of those states to invest, the interest earned on these bonds is tax-free in the state where they're issued. While "munis" offer some tax benefits, they also carry some risk, depending on the creditworthiness of the issuing municipality.

CORPORATE BONDS

Corporate bonds are issued by businesses to raise capital. They have higher yields than government bonds but also carry higher risk.

Bond Risk Levels

If you choose to invest in bonds, you can select your risk level according to your risk tolerance. Here are three options—and you'll note that they align closely to the types of bonds identified above, though individual vehicles should be weighed on their own merits.

LOW-YIELD/LOW-RISK BONDS

The federal government and its agencies back the "safest" debt vehicles, which are US savings bonds, Treasury bonds, and Treasury notes.

MEDIUM-YIELD/MEDIUM-RISK BONDS

Municipal bonds are viewed as medium-risk bonds, and the creditworthiness of the issuing municipality should always be examined.

HIGH-YIELD/HIGH-RISK BONDS

Corporate bonds have a wide range of risk levels. A few trusted credit rating agencies—Fitch, Moody's, and Standard & Poor's—determine the rating of each company's debt, from AAA, meaning "investment grade," down to "junk bond" status. Each agency has its own slightly different scale and process for analysis, but needless to say, the lower the rating on a company's bonds, the higher the interest rate that company will have to offer investors to compensate them for the added risk they are taking. Only you can decide if that reward is worth the risk for you.

Corporate bonds come with four different types of risks:

- **Credit risk:** The company that issued a high-yield bond may perform poorly and not make interest payments as planned, or it may fail and thus default on the bond (also known as *default risk*). Investors could lose their entire principal if that happens. More likely is that, eventually, after a bankruptcy proceeding, bondholders will get some of their money back, but that process can take years, and they won't collect any interest in the meantime.

- **Interest rate risk:** The prevailing interest rates in the market could increase to levels higher than your bonds with longer maturities are paying. If that happens, the market value of your bond will decrease, as it will become a less attractive investment option than other similar ones that are available.

- **Economic risk:** If, as a group, investors in high-yield bonds start viewing them as too risky in a changing economic environment, they may start selling the assets in a flight to safety. The resulting flood of bonds into the market could push the value of your bonds down. In other words, other people's panic can impact the market price of your bond investments.

- **Liquidity risk:** Liquidity, as we've discussed before, simply means the ease and speed with which you can sell a financial asset. For highly liquid assets that trade regularly in large volumes—like investment-grade bonds—finding a buyer when you want to sell is quick and painless. With high-yield junk bonds, it can be harder.

As you can see, the saying "no pain, no gain" holds true here, especially when investing in higher-risk/higher-yield corporate bonds. So pay attention to your risk tolerance level and how quickly you need to access your money.

The Advantages and Disadvantages of Bonds

Before you buy a bond, consider the pluses and the minuses so that you can make the best decision for your money. Let's summarize.

In the plus column:

- Bonds provide investors with a steady income stream through fixed interest payments.
- They are generally considered a lower-risk investment option than equities (stock).
- They are available in various maturities and credit ratings, allowing investors to tailor their bond investments to their needs.
- They can usually be easily bought and sold on secondary markets, providing investors with liquidity.

In the minus column:

- The returns on bonds are generally lower than those of stocks, and may not provide enough growth to outpace inflation.
- The market value of a bond will fluctuate in response to changes in interest rates, credit ratings, and market conditions.
- Because bonds are subject to interest rate risk, their market value may decline if interest rates rise.
- There is always the risk of default, although this risk is generally lower than with equities.

In a nutshell, if you want to diversify your portfolio or you're just starting out as an investor, consider investing in bonds. With almost-guaranteed returns and varied levels of risk to choose from, bonds are the investing equivalent of having your cake and eating it, too.

ALLANISM

Bonds are a good investment for individuals who have a low risk tolerance.

MUST-KNOW FACT 19
When buying a mutual fund, you are investing in a portfolio of stocks, bonds, or other securities.

Many financial innovations, such as the increased availability of low-cost mutual funds, have improved opportunities for households to participate in asset markets and diversify their holdings.
JANET YELLEN, US SECRETARY OF THE TREASURY

Mutual funds have long been popular investment vehicles, and because they are among the most common offerings in employer-sponsored retirement funds such as 401(k)s, they give many people their introduction to the world of investing. They also make it easy to invest in the market, because you don't have to pick individual stocks, bonds, or other securities. In this Must-Know Fact, we'll look at how mutual funds work.

The Basics of Mutual Funds

A *mutual fund* is an investment vehicle that pools money from many investors to purchase a large portfolio of stocks, bonds, or other securities. The returns from the portfolio are shared among the investors, proportional to their investments, minus the fee the fund charges, which is calculated annually as a percentage of the money each investor has in the fund.

Each mutual fund portfolio is managed by a professional fund manager who uses the pooled money to buy a diverse range of assets following an investment philosophy or formula that the fund will make clear in its prospectus, a formal document that provides the details of an investment offering and is filed with the SEC. While the prospectus tells you the focus of the fund, you may not know the fund's exact holdings. Fund managers are required to report the investments held in the portfolio only quarterly.

There are two main types of funds: actively managed funds and index funds.

With an *actively managed fund*, the portfolio manager buys and sells shares in the portfolio's holdings with some frequency as they attempt to ride the trends and deliver the best possible returns. Some funds invest in specific industries—for example, the Vanguard Health Care Fund or the Fidelity Natural Resources Fund. Others invest in stocks that meet a certain set of criteria, based on their in-house research. For instance, the Fidelity Magellan Fund sums up its approach as "invest in companies with market values greater than $10 billion that fund managers believe are poised for growth." So that fund could hold shares of any large-cap companies that its manager believes in.

Index funds, meanwhile, take a much more staid—almost boring—approach. The portfolios they hold more or less match the stocks in a specific index, whether it's the Dow Jones Industrial Average, the NASDAQ Composite, the S&P 500 (these are the three indexes most followed in the media), or a less well-known index like the Russell 2000, which includes about 2,000 of the smallest publicly traded US companies. Managers of these funds aren't attempting to make clever predictions about which stocks will go up or down. They just align their portfolios to the index they track and let the chips fall where they may. Because that's a lot less work, index funds charge lower fees to investors than actively managed funds do.

You might think that the actively managed funds, with their highly paid expert fund managers, would generally beat the passively managed index funds. More often than not, though, they don't. And the longer the time frame you look at, the fewer actively managed funds beat their benchmark indexes, which only serves to highlight the challenge of trying to consistently beat the market through active management.[36]

Types of Mutual Funds and Their Pros and Cons

There are three popular types of mutual funds: equity mutual funds, fixed-income mutual funds, and balanced mutual funds, with pros and cons to each.

EQUITY MUTUAL FUNDS

Equity mutual funds invest primarily in stocks. One reason they're so popular is because they take the hard work out of creating a diversified portfolio. But as discussed above, not all mutual funds are created equal.

Advantages of equity mutual funds:
- There is potential for high returns.
- You get diversification across many stocks.
- The fund has professional management.

Disadvantages of equity mutual funds:
- You have a higher risk of losing your principal than with bond funds.
- Market volatility will lead to fluctuations in returns.
- Management fees can be relatively high, particularly if you pick actively managed funds.

FIXED-INCOME MUTUAL FUNDS

Fixed-income mutual funds invest in bonds and other fixed-income securities, such as Treasury bills, corporate bonds, and municipal bonds. Fixed-income mutual funds are popular because they provide steady income streams with less risk than equity mutual funds. The payout varies from fund to fund as well as within a fund as its managers adjust the portfolio over time, but the returns tend to be higher than the interest you'd get on the average high-yield savings account. The income streams from fixed-income mutual funds vary. Some dividends are paid quarterly, others semi-annually.

Fixed-income mutual funds come with some credit risk, just as other fixed-income vehicles, such as bonds, do. If bond issuers fall into financial trouble and pay their investors back late or, worse, default, they leave their bondholders (you, the investor via the mutual fund) with a bond that's worthless—or worth less than it should have been. However, as with equity mutual funds, by being in a larger pool of investments, the risk is mitigated.

Advantages of fixed-income mutual funds:
- You receive steady income streams.
- There is lower risk than with equity mutual funds.
- You get diversification across multiple types of bonds and fixed-income assets.
- The fund has professional management.

Disadvantages of fixed-income mutual funds:
- Returns are usually weaker than stock returns (in the long run) and will rarely be high.
- Changing interest rates can impact returns.
- Credit risk can affect returns.

BALANCED MUTUAL FUNDS

Balanced mutual funds invest in a mix of stocks and bonds in an effort to balance the fairly secure income streams of fixed-income assets and the growth potential of stocks.

Advantages of balanced mutual funds:

- You get a balanced mix of reliable income and growth potential.
- You get diversification across numerous stocks and bonds.
- The fund has professional management.

Disadvantages of balanced mutual funds:

- Returns may not be as high as pure equity (stock) funds.
- Market volatility will impact returns.
- Management fees can be relatively high.

One more note about mutual funds: When you buy or sell, the transaction takes effect only after the markets close, so you get that day's *closing* price. I mention it here because it will become an important distinction when we discuss exchange-traded funds (ETFs) in Must-Know Fact 20.

Mutual funds can offer both wannabes and seasoned investors professional management and diversification, along with a nice potential for returns. However, before you put your money into one, as with all investments, it's essential to understand the benefits and risks associated with the specific mutual fund, and whether it fits with your investment goals and risk tolerance.

ALLANISM

Invest in assets that you understand.
This includes reading the fine print related
to the asset you intend to purchase.

———————

MUST-KNOW FACT 20
Like mutual funds, exchange-traded funds (ETFs) are portfolios of securities, but they trade like stocks.

Have good trading hygiene. The vast majority of ETFs deliver on their core promise to investors. But if you trade them poorly, that's probably on you.

DAVE NADIG, FORMER CEO OF ETF.COM

———————

Now that we've talked about mutual funds, it's time for me to introduce you to mutual funds' younger sibling: exchange-traded funds (ETFs). As with a mutual fund, an ETF holds a portfolio of stocks and securities, providing instant diversification for your money. But they also have some key differences.

The Basics of Exchange-Traded Funds

The exchange-traded fund first became available as an investment option in 1993, when the SPDR S&P 500 ETF Trust (SPY) was created by State Street Global Advisors and the American Stock Exchange.[37] (In 2008, the NYSE acquired the American Stock Exchange.) As you might guess, this ETF is designed to track the S&P 500 index. Buying shares in it gives you an instantly diversified investment into all 500 of those large US companies.

That ETF—and all those that followed—differed from the previously available mutual funds in some subtle, but profound, ways. As noted in Must-Know Fact 19, with mutual funds, when you want to put money in or take money out, you can do so only after the market closes, with the value of your investment based on the closing prices of the assets in the portfolio. ETFs, on the other hand, trade all session long, just like stocks, and their prices move to reflect the sum of the moves of all the underlying assets in real time.

In the years since that first SPDR appeared, numerous ETFs have been launched: some that also track the S&P 500, some that track the NASDAQ Composite or the Dow, others that follow indexes of the eleven business sectors we explored earlier, and still others that track any number of other indexes with specific focuses. There are also bond ETFs, international ETFs, emerging market ETFs, small-cap ETFs, even crypto sector ETFs—and the list keeps growing.

There are a lot of letters and abbreviations coming your way in the following paragraphs, but humor me—it's necessary if we're going to familiarize you with a couple of the most popular and well-known ETFs.

The Invesco QQQ Trust (NASDAQ: QQQ) tracks the performance of the NASDAQ-100 index, which is made up of 100 of the largest non-financial companies listed on the NASDAQ stock exchange. Also known as the QQQ ETF, its top holdings include Apple, Amazon, and Microsoft. It is considered a growth-oriented ETF because so many of its top holdings are technology companies with high growth potential.

The SPDR Dow Jones Industrial Average ETF Trust (NYSE: DIA), also known as the DIA ETF, tracks the performance of the Dow Jones Industrial Average (DJIA), which is made up of thirty large-cap and mega-cap companies representing various industries. The top holdings of the DIA ETF include Goldman Sachs, UnitedHealth Group, Boeing, and Caterpillar. The DIA ETF is considered a blue-chip ETF because all of its holdings are established, financially stable companies that have been around for decades.

Investors can use these ETFs to gain exposure to their respective indexes and potentially benefit from the performance of the companies in their portfolios. However, it's important to note that, like all investments, these ETFs carry some level of risk, and investors should carefully consider their investment objectives and risk tolerance before investing.

Advantages of Exchange-Traded Funds

Exchange-traded funds have several key benefits:

Diversification. ETFs provide investors with diversification because they hold large baskets of assets, thereby reducing the impact of losses from the performance of individual stocks or bonds. This diversification also helps mitigate market volatility.

Lower fees. ETFs typically have lower expense ratios than traditional mutual funds, because most of them are passively managed and have lower transaction costs. This can lead to significant savings for investors over the long term. However, a growing number of ETFs are actively managed, so pay careful attention when you buy, and don't assume that ETF automatically means passive management and low fees.

Flexibility. This is a big one: ETFs can be bought and sold on the stock market throughout the trading day, allowing investors to enter and exit positions as they see fit. This makes ETFs an excellent option for investors who might want to take advantage of short-term market movements.

Transparency. ETFs must disclose their holdings daily, allowing investors to easily assess their investments. This level of transparency benefits investors who want to ensure that their investments align with their values. Mutual funds, by contrast, generally disclose their holdings just once a quarter, as required by the SEC.

Tax efficiency. ETFs are often more tax-efficient than traditional mutual funds, as they typically have lower share turnover rates, resulting in fewer taxable events.

Disadvantages of Exchange-Traded Funds

While ETFs have some great benefits, they also have downsides to be aware of:

Trading costs. ETFs typically have lower expense ratios than mutual funds, but investors must still pay brokerage commissions when buying and selling ETF shares. These commissions can add up quickly, particularly for frequent traders.

But there are conditions under which you might be able to avoid those commissions: some brokerage houses that offer their own ETFs (and mutual funds) don't charge commissions when you buy and sell them in their in-house accounts. So if, for example, you had an account at Vanguard, you could use it to buy and sell shares of the Vanguard S&P 500 ETF (VOO), and you wouldn't be charged commissions on those transactions. Make the same trades in an account elsewhere, and you would.

Liquidity. While ETFs are traded like individual stocks, not all ETFs are equally liquid. Investors who want to buy or sell a less liquid ETF may have trouble finding buyers or sellers, leading to wider bid-ask spreads and potentially higher trading costs.

Complexity. The basic concept of ETFs is relatively simple, but the proliferation of ETFs in recent years has made the market increasingly complex. As a result, investors have more and more choices, and if they are not careful, they may end up with a product based on underlying assets they don't understand. And you know my advice about investing in something you don't understand . . . Don't.

Volatility. While ETFs provide investors with the benefits of diversification, they are still subject to market volatility. When an entire index sinks, diversification can do only so much to cushion the impact. So investors in ETFs may still experience significant declines during periods of market turbulence.

It's clear there are good reasons ETFs have become popular investment options, but investors should also be aware of the potential drawbacks. And in the end, like mutual funds, ETFs do take a fair amount of control out of the hands of the individual investor.

If you want to take higher risks in pursuit of the higher potential returns you could derive from a more focused stock portfolio—one in which your winning investments could have a bigger impact—ETFs might not be the best choice for you. Ultimately, as with all investment considerations, your decision whether or not to invest in ETFs depends on your risk tolerance and the role you would want them to play in your overall portfolio.

ALLANISM

**You can't have everything.
If you want several stocks in a particular sector,
invest in an ETF that focuses on that sector.**

MUST-KNOW FACT 21
Index funds consistently outperform the large majority of actively managed funds over the long term.

By periodically investing in an index fund, the know-nothing investors can outperform most investment professionals.
WARREN BUFFETT, CO-FOUNDER OF BERKSHIRE HATHAWAY

We've already discussed index funds a bit in the prior two Must-Know Facts, but sometimes important things bear repeating: If you want an investment vehicle that can deliver solid, reliable returns without having to stress over which of the thousands of available stocks to choose, then consider an index fund. My investing guru, Allan, has a great analogy to describe them: "An index fund is like a buffet for your money, where you invest in a little bit of everything without having to choose one main entrée. It's like having a financial all-you-can-eat pass!"

The Basics of Index Funds

As you recall, index funds—whether mutual funds or ETFs—aim to track the performance of a specific index, such as the S&P 500 or the NASDAQ Composite, usually by holding a portfolio that contains each and every stock in that index, in the right proportions. So rather than attempting to beat the market by choosing a few or even a few dozen individual stocks, when you buy an index fund, you invest in *all* the securities that index includes.

Let me give you a concrete example: If you buy shares in an S&P 500 index fund, you would be spreading your investment across all 500 of its companies according to each company's weighted proportion in the index. The S&P 500 is market-cap weighted, so the impact each stock has on the performance of the index is proportional to that company's current value.

If that sounds a little complicated, I bet putting some real numbers to it will make everything clear.

In late 2023, the market cap of the S&P 500—the total market cap of all of its constituent companies—was about $36 trillion. Apple, the largest company in the index, had a market cap of about $2.73 trillion, or about 7% of the total. So 7% was Apple's "weight" in the index, and a fund that aims to track the index would have had 7% of its assets in Apple stock at that time. The same formula can be used to calculate the weight of every other company in the index.

As an index rises or falls, the value of index funds based on it will follow suit.

Advantages of Index Funds

There are several advantages to investing in index funds, and they are similar to those of other investment options we have discussed:

Diversification. Index funds invest in a diversified portfolio of stocks. And, as you learned in Must-Know Fact 12 on diversification, spreading your investments across different asset classes, sectors, and individual stocks reduces your risk by minimizing the impact of any single investment's performance on your portfolio. That may feel less pleasant when one of your investments skyrockets, but you will be pleased by your diversification strategy when one of the stocks in your portfolio drops by double digits.

Low fees. Index funds are passively managed, meaning you don't have a human being picking and choosing the stocks the portfolio holds. For that reason alone, index funds require less research and management than actively managed funds, so they typically have significantly lower annual fees. Thus, more of your money will remain in your investments, where it can grow and compound over the years.

Better performance. In the near term—say, over one-year periods—benchmark index funds outperform most actively managed funds. According to Morningstar,[38] in 2022, just 43 percent of actively managed funds beat their benchmark indexes. Over the longer term, index funds outperform actively managed funds to an even greater degree. This is due to both their low fees and the fact that they track the performance of the broader market. It's tough to beat the market, but index funds make it easy to more or less *tie* the market.

Accessibility. Index funds are widely available and efficient to invest in. Through a single financial asset with low operating costs, you can get exposure to the broader market or a specific sector or segment of it. You can purchase index funds through any broker or online investment platform, and they can be held in tax-advantaged retirement accounts like IRAs or 401(k)s.

Lower taxes. Because index funds sell shares infrequently, they don't get taxed on capital gains as often as actively managed funds do, so their tax expenses—which they pass on to their investors—are lower.

Disadvantages of Index Funds

Of course, every positive has a corresponding downside. Disadvantages of index funds include the following:

Limited upside potential. While index funds are fairly safe and reliable investments, they do not offer the potential for outsized returns that investing in actively managed funds or buying a smaller portfolio of individual stocks would. Index funds are designed to track the performance of the market, so they *can't* outperform it.

Market volatility. While index funds are generally less risky than individual stocks, broad market volatility will still affect them. In a downturn, the value of your index fund will decrease in close proportion to the decline of the broader market.

Tracking errors. While index funds are designed to track the performance of an underlying index, there is always a risk of divergence between the portfolio and the benchmark. This could be due, for example, to differences in the fund's expenses or the index's weighting methodology. Tracking errors can lead to returns that deviate from those of the underlying index (higher or lower).

Passive management. Index funds ride the currents of the market; no one overseeing their holdings is attempting to make regular adjustments to the portfolio in response to events. Because of that, index funds don't adapt much to market cycles or macroeconomic changes. So, for example, if a particular stock or industry starts to underperform, your index fund will keep right on holding that stock and remain invested in that sector, which could potentially drag down your returns.

There are exceptions, however. The indexes themselves do make adjustments to their components, and when indexes change their lineups, the funds that track them do too. For example, the S&P 500 includes 500 of the largest US companies. If a company's market cap drops far enough that it falls out of that category, it will soon be removed from the index and replaced with another. New companies are also added when an S&P 500 company is taken private or merges with another company. In August and September 2023, Lincoln National (LNC), Newell Brands (NWL), and Advance Auto Parts (AAP) all exited the index and were replaced by Blackstone (BX), Airbnb (ABNB), and Kenvue (KVUE). That sort of swap actually happens with some frequency. As a September 2023 article in *Investor's Business Daily* points out, since

2015, 180 companies have exited the S&P 500.[39] That's a lot of turnover for what people think of as a stable index.

Common Indexes that Funds Track

There are many other indexes that funds can track, including regional indexes, sector-specific indexes, and global indexes. Deciding which ones are right for you (if any) depends on your investment objectives and risk tolerance. Some of the most popular indexes that mutual funds and ETFs track include:

- **S&P 500:** This index includes 500 of the largest publicly traded companies in the United States.
- **Dow Jones Industrial Average:** This index features thirty of the largest blue-chip companies in the United States. It is price weighted, not market-cap weighted, so each company's contribution to the Dow's performance is based on the share price, not on the size (market cap) of the company. And unlike some indexes, decisions about which companies should be part of the DJIA are quite subjective. As documentation on the index methodology states, "A stock is typically added only if the company has an excellent reputation, demonstrates sustained growth and is of interest to a large number of investors."[40] Those are great qualities for a company, but not all are easily measured by an objective yardstick.
- **NASDAQ Composite:** This index includes all the companies listed on the NASDAQ stock exchange.
- **Russell 2000:** This index comprises 2,000 US small-cap companies.

If you're interested in investing in an index fund, I encourage you to research sector-specific indexes, global indexes, and regional indexes.

And before investing, weigh the pros and cons of each and how the fund aligns with your risk tolerance level.

ALLANISM

An index fund is like a buffet for your money.

———

MUST-KNOW FACT 22

When the owners of a privately held company want to list its shares on a stock exchange, they hold an initial public offering (IPO)—that is, they "go public."

To make money in stocks you must have the vision to see them, the courage to buy them, and the patience to hold them.
THOMAS WILLIAM PHELPS, INVESTOR, ANALYST, AND AUTHOR

The first publicly traded company was the Dutch East India Company. Formed in 1602 in what is now the Netherlands, the company also had the first initial public offering, or IPO. What's an IPO, you ask? I can answer that question!

Private versus Public Companies

First, let's take a step back and look at private versus public companies. And note that these are simplified descriptions—there are, of course, details and nuances not covered here.

Private companies are those owned by the founders, executive management, and/or private investors. The public (you and me) cannot just buy shares of the company; if there are investors, they must be invited. Because the companies are private, they are not regulated by the Securities and Exchange Commission (SEC) and they are not required to share financial information with the public. (Of course, they are still bound by various other laws and policies.)

Public companies, by contrast, have decided to sell all or part of their business to anyone who wants to buy them. You are already aware that public companies are listed on stock exchanges, and we discussed the requirements to be listed (for a refresher, see Must-Know Fact 3). Public companies are regulated by the SEC, and because they are available for sale to the public, their financial information must be available to the public. As you can imagine, this level of transparency and having to be accountable to public shareholders brings a new level of scrutiny to the business.

So why would a private company decide to go public? Sometimes founders, private equity owners, and early investors take a company public so they can cash out some portion of their stakes and take their profits. Generally, however, companies go public to raise capital for growth. Private companies tend to be smaller than public companies (though to be clear, there are plenty of *enormous* privately held companies), so going public is generally viewed as a significant milestone in a company's development.

What does it take for a company to join the universe of stocks that folks like you and I can invest in? Let's take a look at what's required.

The IPO Process

There are five key steps to an IPO.[41]

Step 1: Finding an underwriter. The company going public establishes a relationship with one or often several underwriters, which are usually investment banks. The main underwriter is responsible for performing due diligence on the company and, together with the issuing company, will determine the price at which shares will be sold to those initial investors on the day of the stock launch.

Step 2: Regulatory filings. The company must file copious paper-work with government regulators to be approved for an IPO. Generating the required documents and financial disclosures for the SEC is a detailed process that can take from six months to a year. Part of the reason the application process is so intricate is that the SEC wants assurance that a business looking to go public has the potential to become profitable and grow its bottom line. It also wants to ensure that enough accurate information about the company is available for investors to make an informed decision about whether or not they want to buy the stock.

Step 3: Pricing. After the IPO is approved, the effective date for the IPO is set and the initial price is determined. This share price reflects what the underwriter views as the correct market capitalization for the company. It's common for IPO shares to be "underpriced" to ensure all available shares sell.

Step 4: Stabilization. After the stock has come to market, it's the underwriter's job to make sure there is a functioning market at a reasonable price. This means if there are imbalances, the underwriter may buy shares at or below the offer price; however, this type of activity only takes place for a short period.

Step 5: Transition. After the stabilization period, the stock is basically bought and sold according to the demands of the market, rather than via any control by the underwriter.

You may have noted in the pricing step that shares are often underpriced initially—and of course, that's where the fast and easy money is—in buying underpriced shares and turning around and selling them at a higher price in a very short amount of time. However, each underwriter is given a fraction of the total stock being issued to sell to its clients, and in almost all cases, those shares are allocated to large institutional investors, wealthy clients of the banks doing the underwriting, and the underwriters themselves. So even if we wannabe investors manage to buy on the day a company goes public, we are not getting "fresh" IPO shares at the nice low offering price; we are buying shares from those *initial* buyers—and they're looking to make a quick profit.

One safeguard is in place though: private shareholders—individuals who bought or were allocated stock in that company before it went public (for example, employees)—are contractually committed to a post-IPO lockup period. During that period, typically for 90 to 180 days following the IPO, those private investors may not sell their shares. This prevents large investors and stakeholders from immediately flooding the market with shares, which could cause instability in the share price and could potentially suggest insider trading.

ALLANISM

Don't fall in love with a stock.

———————

MUST-KNOW FACT 23

IPOs come with the potential for huge reward, but they also come with correspondingly high risk.

*The whole secret to winning big in the stock market
is not to be right all the time, but to lose
the least amount possible when you're wrong.*
WILLIAM J. O'NEIL, FOUNDER OF *INVESTOR'S BUSINESS DAILY*

———————

Investors can get overly excited about an initial public offering and, oftentimes, jump on a company's bandwagon all too quickly from FOMO—fear of missing out. For that reason alone, it's vital to understand both the potential rewards and the risks of investing in an IPO.

If you are not risk-averse, you may be the type who thrives on the excitement of buying an IPO, but please finish reading this Must-Know Fact before even *thinking* about doing so. Basing any investment decision on hype or emotions is a risky move, so before investing in a company that has recently gone public, carefully evaluate its financials, business model, competitive landscape, and growth prospects.

The Rewards of Buying an IPO

There are a few simple potential rewards of buying an IPO:

- You can make a lot of money.

- You can make a lot of money.
- You can make a lot of money.

Well, 'nuff said.

The Risks of Buying an IPO

As tempting as the rewards might be, let's talk realistically about the potential risks of buying shares during an IPO or shares of any newly public company.

What goes up early often comes down. When a company's stock first begins trading, a lot of activity happens in a fairly short window. Enthusiastic buyers rush to place orders, while some of the big players who actually got shares at the IPO price will have set higher ask prices (the prices at which they are willing to sell) with the natural goal of making a profit. Also, the volume of shares available to buy is usually fairly small at that point compared to the entire ownership of the company (i.e., individuals within the company likely hold a large number of the shares at this point). A small "float"—meaning the shares available for sale—often means demand outstrips supply, and the price pops. But those pops don't always last. As of December 20, 2022, 87 percent of the nearly 400 companies that were first listed in 2021 were still trading below their initial offering prices.[42]

Volatility. The stock prices of newly public companies are often volatile, for a number of reasons. Newly public companies do not have a track record of publicly reported business results that you can look at, and often the information that is available doesn't offer ordinary investors enough to go on. For many of these companies, success or failure will rest on a host of factors that are still unclear at the time of the IPO. Will the business model work? Can its technology be manufactured profitably at scale? Will its drug candidates be approved? Unknowns like these can create a roller-coaster ride in share price. And by the time you exit the ride, it's entirely possible that you will have lost part or even all of the money that you invested in that IPO.

Now that you know the risks and rewards of buying an IPO, let me ask you about your risk tolerance level: *Can you handle a lot of risk?*

If you don't think so, then think twice about buying a stock shortly after its IPO.

On the other hand, if you have a high tolerance for risk and are committed to a long-term investment strategy, then you could consider buying an IPO. But before you decide, ask yourself:

- Is the money I will be using to buy these IPO shares "excess cash" rather than money I will need for an upcoming car or house payment? In other words, can I afford to risk it?
- Am I intending to hold these newly issued shares long term? (Reminder: your definition of long term should be a minimum of ten years!)

Just in case I have not been explicit enough about reward and risk, let's look at two case studies of well-known companies that went public.

Case Study: Facebook

Imagine you bought 50 shares of Facebook (now Meta, stock symbol META) when it made its debut on May 18, 2012. As a retail investor (as opposed to an institutional investor), you probably couldn't have purchased this stock at its $38 per share offering price, but if you'd waited until just before the end of its first trading session, you could have bought shares for $38.23, which was the price it closed at that day. Your 50 Facebook/Meta shares cost $1,911.50, and you were committed to holding them for a minimum of ten years.

Table 6 shows what would have happened to your investment during those ten years.

Table 6. Facebook/Meta (META) stock price history, 2012 to 2023

Date	Closing Stock Price	The Value of Your 50 Shares (rounded)
IPO Day—May 18, 2012	$38.23	$1,911
May 1, 2013	$24.35	$1,217
May 1, 2014	$63.30	$3,165
May 1, 2015	$79.19	$3,959
May 1, 2016	$118.81	$5,940
May 1, 2017	$151.46	$7,573
May 1, 2018	$191.78	$9,589
May 1, 2019	$177.47	$8,873
May 1, 2020	$225.09	$11,254
May 1, 2021	$328.73	$16,436
May 1, 2022	$211.13	$10,556
May 1, 2023	$243.12	$12,156

How would you have felt watching the price of your Facebook shares drop from $38.23 to $24.35 in the year after you bought them? It might have been disheartening to see your $1,911.50 investment fall to $1,217.50. And if that sounds painful, consider that $24.35 a share was far from the lowest level those shares touched. On September 4, 2012—not even four months after its IPO—Facebook had lost more than half its value and closed the day at an all-time low of $17.73.

Would you have panicked and sold? Would you have thrown in the towel and cut your losses? Or would you have reminded yourself of your long-term investment strategy of holding the stocks you buy for at least ten years? If you would have sold, then buying IPOs is not for you. If you are a long-term thinker and promised yourself that you would stay the course, then I have some good news for you.

Two years after making your initial investment, your $1,911 would have grown to $3,165. And as you can see from the chart, in the third year, your $1,911 would have grown to $3,959. By having a long-term mindset, you can see that you made a good decision to buy this IPO. That is not the case with every IPO, however. Not all new stocks rise steadily over the long term like Facebook/Meta did. Some go up and down, but some just go down, which is why it's important to do your research before you rush out and buy a newly issued stock.

Case Study: Nvidia

For another scenario, let's look at Nvidia (NVDA), which is my favorite computer chip, networking, and artificial intelligence stock. The company was founded in 1993 and went public on January 22, 1999, at an IPO price of $12 a share.

That stock popped nicely on its first day, closing at $19.69. Let's say that you bought 100 shares for a total investment of $1,969. Now take a look at Table 7 to see how your $1,969 investment would have fared over a twenty-three-year period.

Table 7: Nvidia (NVDA) stock price history, 1999 to 2022

Date	Closing Stock Price	Price (not adjusted for splits)	Value of 100 Shares (not adjusted for splits)
IPO Day— Jan 18, 1999	$19.69	$19.69	$1,969
Dec 27, 1999	$46.94	$46.94	$4,694
Stock splits 2-for-1 on June 27, 2000			
Dec 25, 2000	$32.77	$65.54	$6,554
Stock splits 2-for-1 on September 10, 2001			
Dec 31, 2001	$66.90	$267.60	$26,760
Dec 31, 2002	$11.51	$46.04	$4,604
Dec 31, 2003	$23.20	$92.80	$9,280
Dec 31, 2004	$23.56	$94.24	$9,424
Dec 30, 2005	$36.56	$146.24	$14,624

Date	Closing Stock Price	Price (not adjusted for splits)	Value of 100 Shares (not adjusted for splits)
Stock splits 2-for-1 on April 7, 2006			
Dec 29, 2006	$37.01	$296.08	$29,608
Stock splits 3-for-2 on September 11, 2007			
Dec 31, 2007	$34.02	$408.24	$40,824
Dec 31, 2008	$8.07	$96.84	$9,684
Dec 31, 2009	$18.68	$224.16	$22,416
Dec 31, 2010	$15.40	$184.80	$18,480
Dec 30, 2011	$13.86	$166.32	$16,632
Dec 31, 2012	$12.26	$147.12	$14,712
Dec 31, 2013	$16.02	$192.24	$19,224
Dec 31, 2014	$20.05	$240.60	$24,060
Dec 31, 2015	$32.96	$395.52	$39,552
Dec 30, 2016	$106.74	$1,280.88	$128,088
Dec 29, 2017	$193.50	$2,322.00	$232,200
Dec 31, 2018	$133.50	$1,602.00	$160,200
Dec 31, 2019	$235.30	$2,823.60	$282,360
Dec 31, 2020	$522.20	$6,266.40	$626,640
Stock splits 4-for-1 on July 20, 2021			
Dec 31, 2021	$294.11	$14,117.28	$1,411,728
Dec 30, 2022	$146.14	$7,014.72	$701,472

As you can see, things started off all peaches and cream for shareholders in those first several years following Nvidia's IPO. In fact, at times it was even better than the chart above would suggest: by May 2000, the price had climbed to a peak of almost $113 a share. Your initial investment of $1,969 would have increased in value to almost $11,300.

Then the wheels came off. The dot-com bubble burst and the values of companies in the tech sector—which Nvidia is a part of—sank. The value of your shares would have decreased by around 70% to a low of $3,277.

Let me ask you: *Would your risk tolerance level still be as high as you once thought it was after you experienced that kind of drop in your investment?* After your shares fell in value by more than half, would you have decided to cut your losses while you were at least still in the black, sold, and moved on? I hope not. Remember, a long-term investment strategy means sticking with companies that you believe in enough to buy for at least ten years. Time and patience are two of your biggest allies in stock investing.

On September 17, 2001, Nvidia stock split 2-for-1 for a second time, and shares increased in value to $66.90 as of the last day of the year. That means that your 200 shares would have become 400 shares. That also means that your $1,969 initial investment would have increased to $26,760 in approximately sixteen months (400 shares at $66.90 each). Looking a little better, wouldn't you say?

But remember, young, newly public companies can be volatile, and Nvidia was no exception. The year 2002 was a down year for Nvidia stock, and on December 31, 2002, it was valued at just $11.51 per share. So, the value of your 400 shares would have dropped to $4,604—down more than 80% in a single year. Many investors would have panicked at this point. In fact, a lot of people did.

It took years before Nvidia fully recovered from that slump, and no doubt some short-term thinkers wanted to jump ship in 2003, 2004, and 2005.

But recover it did—and on April 7, 2006, Nvidia performed a *third* stock split. So, your 400 shares would have doubled to 800 shares, and at the close of the session on December 29, 2006, those 800 shares, trading at $37.01, would have been valued at $29,608.

While those first seven years during which you could have owned a piece of Nvidia were volatile, your initial investment of $1,969 would have increased in value more than fifteenfold.

Let's take your Nvidia investment one step further by assuming that you decided to hold on to the stock even longer. If you had, you would have benefited greatly, as Nvidia offered yet a fourth split. This time, however, it was 3-for-2. So that means that your 800 shares of Nvidia would have increased to 1,200 shares. And then, years later, after climbing to a high just above $800 a share, it split again 4-for-1. While you're jumping for joy (and with reason!), I want you to know that your $1,969 initial investment would have grown—after twenty-one years, as of the end of 2021, to a value of $1,411,728!

But even a passing glance at the ups and downs of that stock price table shows just how much Nvidia fluctuated on the way to that life-changing investment return. The chipmaker is, after all, a cyclical stock (as we discussed in Must-Know Fact 2).

"Okay," you may be saying, "I'm convinced that buying an IPO stock is not for the faint of heart." You are right about that. However, you should also be able to see that if you think long term, there is a chance that you could reap big rewards from doing so.

If you had been able to look into a crystal ball at the end of 2007, and learned only that Nvidia's stock prices were going to be fairly volatile between 2008 and 2014, what do you imagine you would have done?

1. Kept all of your shares of Nvidia and waited it out?
2. Sold enough shares to cash out your initial $1,969 investment and kept your gains in shares of Nvidia?
3. Jumped ship entirely because you'd had it with all the volatility?

While there is no right or wrong answer to this question in the abstract, in the specific case of Nvidia, you would have made a healthy profit no matter which option you chose.

If you'd chosen option 1 and kept your 1,200 shares of Nvidia, they would have become 4,800 shares following the 4-for-1 split on July 20, 2021. By the end of 2021, your 4,800 shares of Nvidia at $294.11 per share would have been valued at $1,411,728. Yes! A long-term investment strategy pays off! And that amount does not even include the dividends that the company started paying in 2013. But as they say, the only constant is change. By the end of December 2022, those 4,800 shares of Nvidia would have been valued at $806,400—down more than 40% in the space of a year. Granted, that's a big drop. Yet you would still have a holding worth vastly more than your initial investment of $1,969.

If you'd chosen option 2 and decided to sell shares worth approximately your initial investment of $1,969 from your Nvidia holdings of $24,060 on December 31, 2014, and then played with "the house's money," you would have sold 98 shares, leaving you 1,102 shares in your portfolio. If you had held on to those shares, on July 20, 2021, they would have increased to 4,408 shares thanks to the 4-for-1 split. And as of the end of 2022, they would have grown in value to $644,185.12. Not too shabby!

If you'd chosen option 3 and jumped the Nvidia ship by selling your 1,200 shares in December 2007 when they were priced at $34.02, your proceeds would have been $40,824—more than 20 times what you paid in 1999.

So, there you have it. The choice to buy IPOs or not is entirely up to you, but if you choose to do so, please make sure to do your research, only invest what you consider to be excess cash, and have the patience to hold on to the stock for a minimum of ten years.

ALLANISM

Buying stocks based on emotion can be very costly.

———

MUST-KNOW FACT 24
It is essential to do comprehensive research before buying cryptocurrency.

What value does cryptocurrency actually add?
No one's been able to answer that question for me.
STEVE EISMAN, PORTFOLIO MANAGER

———————
———————

The first time I heard the term *cryptocurrency*, I was confused by the concept and how it worked. (People use computers to "mine" digital money? It's "money," but not backed by any government?)

Allan, my language-of-investing guru, reminded me of an important guideline that wise investors follow: It's best to invest in what you understand, because a knowledgeable investor is a powerful investor.

As of this book's publication, I've taken his advice and avoided investing in crypto. I've learned the basics, but from my perspective, I'd need to learn a lot more before I'd be in a position to make properly informed decisions about putting my money into this new form of asset.

Some financial experts see crypto as the future of money. It may or may not be. I'm sure many individuals experienced the same hesitation when Western Union became one of the first organizations to roll out the credit card concept in 1914. Back then, people referred to these strange new payment methods as "metal money." It was unheard of for merchants to offer credit to people they didn't personally know and trust, and at first, the credit card option was only offered to a small number of customers.[43]

Whether you choose to buy cryptocurrency or not is your decision, of course. These assets could be part of a broad, diversified portfolio, or you might decide to wait and see how this asset class does in the coming years before putting your real, hard-earned dollars into virtual currencies.

Now, as I've already said, I'm no crypto expert. There are plenty of online resources that can go into greater depth than I can about the ins and outs of crypto, but in the interest of being thorough, I'll cover some of the basics here.

How Cryptocurrencies Work

The fundamental concept of a cryptocurrency was introduced in a white paper published in 2008 by someone using the pseudonym Satoshi Nakamoto. Titled "Bitcoin: A Peer-to-Peer Electronic Cash System," it outlined the basic principles of a new type of currency that would be digital, decentralized, and secure. When Nakamoto—whoever they really are—launched the Bitcoin protocol in January 2009, the first globally viable cryptocurrency was born.

At its core, *cryptocurrency* is a digital medium of exchange. Just as you might use a debit card, a credit card, or an online payment system such as Zelle or PayPal to pay digitally for a purchase, you can also use a cryptocurrency to buy something (assuming the other party accepts that type of cryptocurrency as a payment option).

Cryptocurrencies are decentralized digital assets that rely in part on cryptography—that is, encoded communications—for their security. In this context, "crypto" refers to the unique systems of encrypting and decrypting information that secure all the transactions and data sent between users of the cryptocurrency.

An individual unit of crypto is called a *coin* or a *token*. You'll never see a physical Bitcoin or Dogecoin, only digital images that represent the coins. Tokens can be moved from one person's possession to another, just as you might transfer cash from your checking account to someone else's via a digital transaction. These transfers usually take place via peer-to-peer networks, and transactions can be completed faster than ordinary bank transactions, particularly when it comes to cross-border exchanges, where traditional methods are slow.

No single entity—for example, a bank—tracks who has which tokens. Instead, the information is recorded on a *blockchain*, a distributed, digital ledger. Many copies of that ledger are stored on servers run by independent entities, and each time a validated transaction occurs, all the ledgers get updated. This prevents any single ledger-holder from engaging in fraud, but it doesn't always prevent fraudsters and hackers from digitally stealing cryptocurrencies.

As a result of de facto anonymity and the loose regulation inherent in cryptocurrency, it has emerged as a preferred transaction technology for users engaged in criminal activity. Issues of money laundering, tax evasion, and illicit transactions on the dark web have yet to be addressed as governments and regulators struggle to catch up.[44]

The Value of Cryptocurrency

Do you remember when the US dollar was backed by gold? (Some of you might not!) When a currency is backed by an asset or commodity, such as gold, it is termed a *representative currency*. When the value of the commodity backing it rises or falls, so does the value of the currency. However, since 1971 the US dollar has been what is called a *fiat currency*, which means there is no asset backing it. The value of a fiat currency comes instead from the backing of the national government and central bank of the country issuing it. Between them, the government and bank control the money supply and the country's fiscal policies, which gives them some influence over how much their currencies will be worth. Other fiat currencies include the rupee, the yen, and the euro.

Cryptocurrencies are neither fiat currencies nor representative currencies. The value of a cryptocurrency rises and falls based partly on the market's demand for it, but perhaps even more so based on the emotions of crypto traders. In this regard, cryptocurrencies are something like stocks. But unlike stocks, there are no real businesses directly underlying their value. With cryptos, there are no profits for shareholders to share in, nor revenues from any sales.

However, each cryptocurrency does have a network, and in some cases, software developers use those networks and tokens to support their applications. If an application proves useful for people and businesses, and using it requires tokens of a specific type, demand will rise for those tokens. But to a greater degree than with assets that are tied to something more tangible, the valuation of any particular cryptocurrency will be heavily based on speculation.

Additionally, while cryptocurrencies function as money, they get no FDIC protection. Recall that if you deposit ordinary US dollars in a traditional FDIC-insured bank and that bank fails, the government will make sure you get your money back—up to $250,000 per account per ownership category. Numerous cryptocurrency-affiliated companies—FTX, Genesis Global Capital, BlockFi, and others—have gone bust in recent years. Many investors with holdings in cryptocurrencies have seen those assets frozen.[45] They may get some of their money back eventually, but they will certainly take some losses, possibly steep ones.

Cryptocurrency Mining and Minting

As I noted earlier, cryptocurrency operates on a blockchain, a decentralized and distributed ledger. When someone performs a transaction, the ledger is updated, and the way to ensure the data integrity and security is known as the *consensus mechanism*. That is, it is necessary to validate that transactions are legitimate, from creation to confirmation. The most common consensus mechanisms are *proof of work (PoW)* and *proof of stake (PoS)*. Since you may have heard these terms, I'll give a *very* basic explanation.

Proof of work, or *cryptocurrency mining*, involves solving extremely complex cryptographic math problems that validate a block of transactions before they are added to the ledger. The problems are so difficult that the only method that works is brute force: a random (but possible) answer is generated and tested to see if it works; the process is repeated until a solution is found. *Miners*—who could be individuals, groups, or companies—use high-power computers to attempt to solve these problems. The first miner to solve the problem, thus validating the block, is rewarded with new coins or tokens. Each block of transactions must be validated in this manner before it is added to the blockchain. Bitcoin is a good example of a cryptocurrency that uses PoW.

Among the problems with a proof-of-work protocol is that it's extremely energy intensive. Those computers, all running hot as they perform complex computations in search of valid solutions, suck down an absurd amount of power. The University of Cambridge reports that in 2022, Bitcoin mining used 124.5 terawatt hours of electricity—about as much as all of Argentina, a country of 45 million people.

The upshot is that of the 22,000-plus cryptocurrencies now in existence, barely over 100 use PoW. The majority instead rely on *proof of stake*, where the addition of a block to the blockchain is known as *cryptocurrency minting* or *cryptocurrency forging*. In proof of stake, those who wish to earn the rewards (new tokens) for validating transactions must deposit (stake) a significant number of tokens of their own for the privilege. At intervals, those validators' computers will be tasked to be part of a group checking the validity of a set of transactions. Attempting to put false information on the blockchain when you're being trusted to only do what's right risks forfeiting the cryptocurrency you've deposited—your stake. Because PoS engages significantly fewer validators and relies on a more efficient consensus mechanism, it requires less computing power, making it the more energy-efficient method.

I am curious to see how crypto technology evolves in the areas of both environmental sustainability and fraud protection.

The Largest Cryptocurrencies by Market Cap Today

You may wonder why there are so many cryptocurrencies. Lyle Daly, in an article for The Motley Fool, offers this simple explanation: "The biggest reason is there's practically no barrier to entry. Anyone who wants to create a cryptocurrency can do it. Even with *zero* technical know-how, you could hire someone on Fiverr (NYSE: FVRR) to make a cryptocurrency for less than $20!"[46]

But let's focus on some of the cryptocurrencies you're likely to hear of. Table 8 lists the ten largest cryptocurrencies by market cap as of January 5, 2024.

Table 8. Largest cryptocurrencies by market cap as of Jan 5, 2024 (Slickcharts.com)

Cryptocurrency	Market Cap
Bitcoin (BTC)	$860.0 billion
Ethereum (ETH)	$269.9 billion
Tether (USDT)	$92.9 billion
BNB (BNB)	$48.3 billion
Solana (SOL)	$43.4 billion
XRP (XRP)	$30.9 billion
USDC (USDC)	$25.1 billion
Cardano (ADA)	$19.2 billion
Avalanche (AVAX)	$13.5 billion
Dogecoin (DOGE)	$11.8 billion

The top ten list changes fairly regularly, depending on the latest news driving various crypto prices, but Bitcoin and Ethereum are secure in their spots as the two most popular cryptocurrencies by far. The third largest, Tether, is a so-called "stablecoin"—designed to stay exactly equal in value to $1. Tether is something of a "waystation"; people use it for transactions in which they are spending one type of crypto to buy another, or when they are preparing to buy crypto with fiat currencies.

How to Set Up a Cryptocurrency Account

While I am not advocating that you buy cryptocurrency, if you choose to invest in an asset, my goal is to educate you on how to do so. So, start by setting up an account. There are several options for doing so, but Coinbase (coinbase.com) and Robinhood (robinhood.com) are two popular options. Either will allow you to buy, sell, receive, and store a number of cryptos, among them Bitcoin, Ether, and Litecoin.

If you connect those accounts to your traditional bank account, it's relatively simple to convert digital currencies into cash. Some companies are now accepting certain cryptocurrencies as payment, but whether they will ever become as broadly accepted or as widely used as traditional currencies remains to be seen.

When you set up your account, you get two keys: a public key and a private key. The *public key* allows you to receive cryptocurrency from others, and you can share it freely. The *private key* lets you access the funds in your crypto account. This key is similar to the password or sign-in code you use to access your banking and brokerage accounts (though much more complex than any password you might pick yourself), and just as you wouldn't share those login credentials publicly, you don't want to share your private key.

While the private key offers strong security, it is also the single way of gaining access to your assets. Whoever holds the private key can access and use all the crypto associated with it, so *the one thing you don't want to do is lose your key*. If you somehow misplace your key (perhaps by saving it in a secure file that you lose your password for), you're out of luck. It's estimated that 20 percent of all Bitcoin holders are locked out of their accounts, and thus will never be able to recover access to their cryptocurrency because they lost or forgot their keys.[47] And if someone else gets ahold of your key, they can abscond with your crypto, and you'll have more or less no recourse.

In summary, exploring cryptocurrencies requires a mix of curiosity and caution. Whether you choose to dive into the cryptocurrency world or not, understanding this investing landscape is crucial. Cryptocurrencies come with challenges like volatility, fraud risk, and energy usage, and only the future will show how these issues get addressed.

Whether cryptocurrencies become widespread or remain fairly niche, the journey of learning continues, helping investors make informed choices in a changing financial world.

ALLANISM

If it sounds too good to be true, it probably is!

———————

MUST-KNOW FACT 25

Managing your own portfolio requires monitoring it regularly and periodically rebalancing your assets.

Before you can become a millionaire,
you must learn to think like one.
THOMAS J. STANLEY, AUTHOR AND RESEARCHER

———————

By now, you have a general understanding of how the stock market works, what the various types of stock offer, and the benefits of investing in the stock market. When you take the next step of actually investing, you have a decision to make. Will you:

A. Manage your own investment portfolio?
B. Work with a financial advisor?
C. Use a robo-advisor?
D. Use a combination of the options above?

Before you decide, let me give you a few facts that may influence your decision. In this Must-Know Fact, we'll talk about managing your own portfolio, or *self-directed investing*, and in the next two Must-Know Facts, we'll discuss financial advisors and robo-advisors.

According to the March 2019 *Invest in You Savings Survey* conducted by CNBC and Acorns, 75 percent of respondents said they managed their finances without help from a professional or online service. Let me say that again: Three-quarters of all Americans manage their own finances. To me, that's a scary statement, considering that the majority of Americans have never been exposed to a financial literacy class. Only 17 percent of the individuals surveyed said they work with a financial advisor.[48] It won't surprise you that the percentage is lower among younger people, who are on the front end of their financial journey and typically have fewer assets to manage: only 7 percent of respondents age 25 to 34 were using a professional advisor, and a mere 4 percent of those age 18 to 24 were. Conversely, it may not surprise you that 31 percent of respondents age 65 and up said they do have a financial advisor,[49] presumably because they have more assets to consider and are facing the complexities and tax implications that come with retirement.

If you choose to manage your own portfolio, recognize that there are responsibilities associated with it, including being diligent about reviewing the performance of your stock on an ongoing basis. You should also periodically rebalance your portfolio based on your risk tolerance level. This is where having a relationship with a financial advisor can come in handy.

Some new investors may have the false impression that managing their own portfolio is simply a matter of choosing which stocks to buy. They do not recognize the need to plan ahead for future income and the impact of taxes when selling stocks. If you do not have an investing guru in your life, read about investing regularly, take advantage of webinars that your brokerage firm offers, and meet with a financial advisor and/or tax professional on an ongoing basis (or at least annually).

Benefits of Self-Directed Investing

Granted, there are benefits of managing your own portfolio:

Control. Many investors take comfort in having complete autonomy over how and when their money gets invested. (If you like to be the boss of things, this is a huge benefit!)

Access. By choosing what to invest in yourself, you have access to a wider range of investments than what someone else might choose to buy for your portfolio. This benefit lets you explore more, which may be appealing to those of us who are adventurous.

Lower fees. By managing your own portfolio, you avoid paying fees to an advisor. This translates into your having more money available to work for you!

Education. Self-directed investing promotes self-directed learning in the world of stock investing—and this can be a fun, lifelong journey.

But you know what's coming next . . .

Pitfalls of Self-Directed Investing

Now let's look at some of the potential pitfalls of managing your own portfolio.

First let's be clear: no investor wants to intentionally mismanage their money. Oftentimes, they simply have not been exposed to the knowledge about how to invest—or for that matter how to manage money generally. That is, in fact, a main reason that more states are mandating high school students complete a course in financial literacy before they graduate.

Many individuals have not acquired a long-term money mindset in our world of instant gratification. When we're hungry, we place an order on an app or throw something in the microwave. Voilà! Within minutes, we're eating. If we want a new pair of shoes or groceries, we find what we want online, order, and have those things winging their way to our door in short order.

That pursuit of instant gratification has also made it natural for us to assume that there is "fast money" out there, just waiting to be put in our bank account. News media and social media like to feed us stories about the stock traders who got lucky by buying and selling at just the right time, or the people who gambled the lion's share of their savings on a niche cryptocurrency that surged and made them millionaires.

Stories like these can make it easy to conclude that careful, long-term investing is not the approach for you. But beware: You may be falling victim to a logical fallacy called *survivorship bias*. You're looking only at the cherry-picked tales of those who did well with these risky, short-term strategies—and not being shown the far more common stories of those who didn't.

While it's true that you can profit in the short term with self-directed investing, your gains are likely to be exponentially greater in the long term if you simply practice patience. If you want short-term gratification, you might as well go to the local casino and put your money down at the roulette table.

Because many individuals lack financial literacy and a long-term mindset, there are five common mistakes they tend to make when investing without guidance:

- Not identifying the length of time they'll need to reach their financial goal.
- Not figuring out the amount they will need to earn from their investments to achieve their long-range goal.
- Not mapping out the dollar amount they will need to invest monthly to take proper advantage of dollar-cost averaging. (See Must-Know Fact 33.)
- Not being realistic about their risk tolerance level.
- Lack of familiarity with the products and services represented by the stocks.

As my financial literacy guru taught me early on, although to err is human, the better strategy is to learn from the mistakes of others so you can refrain from making them yourself. And when you make an investment mistake (and you will), avoid thinking of what you "should have" done but rather think of any loss as the cost of your "tuition."

Six Criteria for Being a Self-Directed Investor

If you are considering managing your own investments, be sure that you meet these six criteria:

1. You have an emergency fund that could cover a minimum of three to six months' worth of your expenses.
2. You are willing and able to leave the money you invest in those investments for a minimum of five to ten years.
3. You have a passion for learning about the stock market.
4. You have the time to manage your portfolio.
5. You possess a logical mindset.
6. You have a moderate to high risk tolerance.

If you meet the six prerequisites, then you may be ready to be in full control of your investments. However, if you feel iffy about one or more of them, managing your investment portfolio with the counsel of a professional advisor may be a more prudent choice for you. For instance, if you like the idea of paying fewer fees and prefer to make your own decisions, yet you do not have an iota of interest in learning how the stock market works, then managing your own portfolio is probably not the best option. To manage your portfolio effectively, you must be an educated and informed investor.

In my opinion, self-directed investors need one more crucial component to be successful: You must have a stock market guru in your life! While I recognize that you cannot snap your fingers to make a personal stock market guru like Allan appear, you *can* subscribe to investment advisories, attend virtual investment seminars, and listen to podcasts about investing (notice I didn't say podcasts about *trading*—you'll be better served by increasing your investing knowledge before getting into the particulars of trading). I would also urge you to read books by Warren Buffett, William J. O'Neil (the founder of *Investor's Business Daily*), Benjamin Graham, and other investment sages. You will also benefit greatly from analysts' reports. Two of my favorite sources are Morningstar and The Motley Fool, which are both written in easy-to-understand language. You will find a list of recommended books and podcasts at the end of this book.

A Self-Directed Investor's Cautionary Tale

Before you decide to start managing your own portfolio, let me share a story about a guy I'll call Joe. When we met in early 2008, he was adamant about his desire to manage his investments. (The term "adamant" should give you a hint about one of the hurdles Joe faced.)

When we spoke, he told me that he managed his investment portfolio, and, retired from his career, he treated investing as a full-time job, dedicating thirty-five hours each week to watching CNBC, reading investment advisors, and attending investment seminars. While dedicating that amount of time to your investments may sound extreme, I can tell you one thing: he was passionate about the stock market.

Joe's first mistake was putting all his eggs in one basket. Prior to my meeting him, Joe had so fervently believed in Apple stock that he put all of his investable cash into it and bought 2,200 shares—rather than diversifying his portfolio as one financial advisor had encouraged him to do.

Joe did meet several of the six criteria for being a self-directed investor:

- He had an emergency fund set up (1).
- He had a passion for staying informed about stock market trends. He educated himself daily about the investing world by watching a financial news channel. Joe thirsted for stock mar-

ket knowledge and made it a point to stay current about what was happening in the market (3).

- He had the time to focus on managing his investments (4).

But the important criteria that Joe lacked proved critical shortly after he bought all that Apple stock. Joe had a low risk tolerance (6), which caused him to make emotional decisions rather than logical ones (5).

What happened to expose Joe's lack of intestinal fortitude? The 2007–2009 bear market.

Between October 2007 and March 2009, the S&P 500 index slid further and further downward—by 57% to be exact.[50] Though Apple didn't follow precisely the same path down, it fell by a similar percentage from its peak in that period. And Joe lost his nerve.

Apple closed at $194.84 a share (before its split-adjusted amount) on January 2, 2008. On that day, Joe's position of 2,200 shares was valued at $428,648. Fast-forward to January 2, 2009, when the stock closed at $90.75 (before its split-adjusted amount). His portfolio's value was down to $199,650. That was a loss of $228,998 in a single year.

Watching his entire portfolio lose more than half of its value caused Joe to panic. Worried that he could lose even more, early in 2009, he chose to "cut his losses" and sell.

While we all know that hindsight is clearer than foresight, what Joe didn't realize in that moment is that if he had remained logical and calm, and thought about the reasons he had picked Apple in the first place— and then just sat on his hands and done nothing—twelve months later (which admittedly could have felt like an eternity to a person with low risk tolerance), his Apple stock would have recouped the value it had lost, and then some.

Unfortunately, Joe refused to listen to a financial advisor friend who recommended that he stay the course. That friend told Joe that if he didn't need the money he had invested in the next five years, he would be best served by keeping it in the market. Even though Joe's investment statement would show a big loss in January 2009, the only way he would *actually* lose money was if he sold the stock.

Rather than listening to his friend, Joe sold his Apple stock. It didn't take him long to regret his decision.

On January 4, 2010, Apple was trading at $214.01 a share. If Joe had kept his Apple shares rather than selling them, they would have been worth $470,822.

On January 3, 2011, Apple had risen to $329.57 a share. Joe's 2,200 Apple shares would have been valued at $725,054.

And on January 4, 2012, Apple was priced at $411.23 a share. If Joe had kept his 2,200 Apple shares, they would have been valued at $904,706—well more than double his initial investment.

You can do your own calculations to determine how much Joe's shares of Apple would have grown in the ensuing years had he not sold them, but let's just say the math only gets more depressing from here.

(Note: Shares above are not adjusted for share splits, and dollar amounts do not reflect Apple's dividend payments. On June 9, 2014, Apple shares split 7-for-1, which, as you'll remember from the section on stock splits, means that the share price was divided by 7, but the number of shares investors held was multiplied by 7. And on August 31, 2020, Apple split again, this time 4-for-1. Most of the commonly used stock websites handle historical data by giving the split-adjusted prices for periods prior to splits. So recognize that if you're checking, for example, the Yahoo! Finance price for Apple, it reflects Joe's original 2,200 shares as the 61,600 shares he'd have now—worth more than $10.5 million as of September 30, 2023.)

Obviously, letting his investment sit would have *greatly* benefited Joe. But don't take the wrong lesson from the fact that he happened to pick—and then flee—one of the best stocks of the twenty-first century. If he had diversified—let's say, by putting his money into an S&P 500 index fund—he might not have been as likely to panic after that terrible

2008. Truth be told, however, while Joe may have felt safer with his investments spread across 500 stocks, he would still have seen a major drop in the stock market. And like Apple stock, an S&P 500 index fund would have recovered in time.

To this day, Joe regrets his decision to sell his Apple stock. And unfortunately, his low risk tolerance has kept him from returning to the stock market. Instead, he has put his money into a savings account, where the interest it earns isn't even keeping up with inflation.

What would you have done if you had been in Joe's situation after that steep, yearlong market drop? Take your answer into careful consideration when deciding if you really want to manage your investment portfolio entirely on your own, or if you'd be better off working with a professional who can guide you through the pitfalls, point you toward stocks and assets that suit you, help you avoid emotional decisions, and keep your focus on the long term.

ALLANISM

**There are no "should haves."
Think of your investment mistakes as your tuition.**

———————

MUST-KNOW FACT 26
When choosing a financial advisor, two important considerations are how they get paid and whether or not they are a fiduciary.

Everyone lives by selling something.
ROBERT LOUIS STEVENSON,
POET, NOVELIST, AND ESSAYIST

———————
————

Now that you have read about what it takes to manage your investments, I hope you've evaluated whether you have the time, interest, risk tolerance, and mindset to begin your investment journey. If you do, terrific! However, if you are concerned that you might come up short on any of those fronts, there is absolutely nothing wrong with deciding to get some experienced professional help in managing your money. With a professional, you have access to financial counsel, assistance in creating a financial roadmap, and regularly scheduled check-ins to discuss the progress you've made toward your goals.

How can you know which type of advisor and which individual advisor will be the most appropriate choice for you? As with other decisions regarding your investments, there are several factors to consider. One of the most important, in my view, is whether or not the advisor you are considering is a fiduciary.

What It Means to Be a Fiduciary

A *fiduciary* is an individual or company who has a legal duty to act on a client's behalf and to put the client's interest ahead of their own. With a financial advisor who is a fiduciary, we are of course talking about financial advice and investment decisions.

According to the law as explained by the Securities and Exchange Commission, financial fiduciaries have two main duties to their clients:[51]

A Duty of Care. They are obligated to understand each client's financial situation, so that they can make informed recommendations that suit that client. This means they must be well informed not just about the investment choices they are offering, but also the available alternatives, so that they can make recommendations and take actions that are in their clients' best interests. They are required to seek the best execution of transactions (for example, when making trades for a client) so that they maximize value for the client (however, note that maximizing value is not just about minimizing cost). And they are obligated to provide advice and monitoring over the course of the relationship at appropriate frequency for the client.

A Duty of Loyalty. Fiduciaries are not allowed to use their positions to further their own interests at the expense of their clients' interests—for example, by recommending that you put money into an asset that offers them a large commission, but that isn't really right for you. This duty also entails providing transparency around any conflicts of interest and disclosures about when they are acting in a brokerage capacity and when in an advisory capacity.

You can verify a fiduciary financial advisor's credentials on sites like NAPFA.org (The National Association of Personal Financial Advisors) and the Securities and Exchange Commission's advisor database.[52] The SEC takes fiduciary mismanagement seriously—practitioners can lose their license if they don't abide by the rules. If you have doubts about a potential advisor's qualifications, you can request that the person sign a fiduciary oath.[53]

Determining What Type of Advisor You Need

Finding the right financial advisor for you is likely to take some work. This is a professional relationship that you're starting, and as with any relationship, you're going to want to find someone with whom you are simpatico—someone who understands what you want and also what you need, whose communication style doesn't grate on you, and who explains things in a way that you understand. And most of all, someone you feel you can trust to have your best interests at heart.

These professionals do *not* fall into a one-size-fits-all category. With that in mind, I wouldn't advise you to just go with the first advisor you meet or to randomly pick one from the Google or Yelp search results for "financial advisors near me."

Here are four questions to help you decide which type of expert would be best for you.

1. Do you need counsel on how to buy specific products such as stocks, mutual funds, or ETFs? Do you also want broader advice about how to map out your long-term goals, and how to develop a plan that could help you achieve them?

If you answered yes to both questions, then you might be looking for a *financial advisor*. Some advisors are *fee-only advisors*, so you pay them either a flat fee, by the hour, or by a percentage of the assets they manage for you. These professionals are fiduciaries.

Other advisors may be *fee-based* advisors. You do pay them, but they will also earn fees and commissions based on the products they sell to you. The legal standards for their conduct are not as strict as those that apply to fiduciaries.[54]

2. Are you seeking an investment expert who will help you with

your overall financial position by assisting you in creating a budget, creating a savings plan for your children's education, understanding your tax burden and how to reduce it, crafting an estate plan, or managing an inheritance?

If these are things you need help with, you may want a *financial planner* or *wealth manager* who has earned the Certified Financial Planner (CFP) designation. All CFPs are also fiduciaries. A financial advisor helps clients with services like budgeting, saving for retirement, investing, and other aspects of managing their finances. Wealth managers provide financial planning and investment management services to individuals with high net worth. They help clients with short- and long-term financial goals, tax planning, and estate planning.

3. Are you interested in developing a relationship with a financial expert who will focus strictly on helping you buy and sell stocks profitably?

If so, you may be looking for a *broker*. Brokers are not fiduciaries. Their role is to help you with your transactions. They get paid for their work via trading fees, transaction fees, and asset management fees.

They can give you advice about which purchases to make, as long as they guide you toward those that are "suitable" for you. But the suitability standard, as it turns out, is broad, and not as stringent as a fiduciary responsibility.

4. Are you looking for a financial professional with whom you can establish a long-term relationship to help you build your portfolio and then manage it for you, making trades independently?

If so, you want a *portfolio manager*. These professionals may hold various certifications—they might be a CFP, for example. Rather than being paid by commission, they get paid an hourly rate, an annual fee, or an amount based on the percentage of assets they manage for you.[55] And, yes, they are obligated to act as fiduciaries.

No matter which type of investment professional you choose, you should know that Certified Financial Planners (CFPs) and Registered Investment Planners (RIAs) are held to the highest fiduciary standard by the SEC. They are legally bound to put their clients' needs ahead of their own financial interests.

HOW ADVISORS GET PAID

When considering a financial advisor, ask them how they get paid. If they are a fiduciary, you will likely hear one of these answers:

- "I get paid based on the assets under management." Translation: The person charges a percentage of the value of your portfolio.
- "I get paid on retainer." Translation: You will pay a fee, typically quarterly or annually, for all services rendered.
- "I get paid on commission." Translation: The person receives compensation based on the number of trades that are transacted.
- "I get paid an hourly rate." Translation: You'll be charged by the hour for services rendered.

Advisors who are not fiduciaries may get paid through commissions, on a billable-hour basis, or on an advisory fee basis. They also may be given a financial incentive for making recommendations about certain products.

No matter which response you hear, and especially if you are working with someone who is not a fiduciary, make certain to ask about the specific fees and get the fee schedule in writing.

Finding Your Individual Expert

After you have identified your specific needs and the type of expert who can meet them, your next step will be to find one who's right for you.

There's plenty of advice out there about how to pick a financial professional, but I particularly like the advice that CPA Lance Cothern gave on MoneyUnder30.com (one of my favorite websites).[56] He suggests that the best way to begin is to search through databases of vetted professionals such as the one created by Paladin Research and Registry. He also recognizes the value of asking trusted friends and family members for referrals. Remember, though—just because someone you know has had a good experience with an advisor does not mean that person will be the right fit for your financial needs.

From there, make a list of the financial experts who look like they fit your criteria, and then schedule in-person, phone, or video meetings with each of them. Don't just hire the first person you talk to. Interview each one to determine whether the relationship will be a good fit.

QUESTIONS TO ASK A FINANCIAL EXPERT

In your interview have a prepared list of questions. Here are nine you can ask—and of course, add any others you have. You might even email these to the candidate requesting them to respond *before* your scheduled appointment.

1. What do you specialize in? Rather than just telling the person what you need, ask them about their areas of expertise. The responses will help you qualify or disqualify them.

2. Are you a fiduciary? As noted previously, in most cases, you should be getting your advice from someone who is legally obligated to put your interests first. In some cases, an advisor may be a fiduciary for only some of the services they provide. So have them be clear—are they never, always, or only sometimes a fiduciary?

3. How do you get paid? Some financial experts fall into the fee-only category while others also earn commissions based on third-party sales commissions.

4. Are there other costs I'll have to pay beyond your standard fees? If you are seeking tax advice from a financial advisor, you may want to ask if any of their work is ever outsourced to other professionals who will also charge you. You'll be happy that you asked before receiving unexpected bills.

5. Can you provide references from your list of existing clients? Since you may be establishing a long-term relationship with this financial advisor, it's worth hearing what some of their current clients think about them. While those comments may assist you in making a decision, don't place too much stake in them. The advisor will no doubt choose clients who will praise them. (I'm sure that Bernie Madoff's clients spoke highly of him, too, unaware until it was too late that he was running the largest Ponzi scheme in history.)

6. How would you describe your average client? If you're a young adult, you may want a financial advisor whose client base largely matches your profile. If, on the other hand, retirement is looming large on the horizon for you, make sure that the person you are interviewing is familiar with the needs of clients who are planning to soon enter their golden years.

7. What clearinghouses and custodial firms do you use? Clearinghouses such as Charles Schwab, Pershing, and Fidelity Institutional Wealth serve as bridges between broker-dealers and investors. Custodial firms such as Pershing and Fidelity Institutional Wealth are institutions that retain the securities of clients. (As you see, these firms can act as both a clearinghouse *and* a custodial firm.) By asking this question, you will learn which reputable organization holds clients' assets and processes the transactions on behalf of the financial advisor. Even within the same parent firm, the services and the pricing may be different. You may want to ask questions related to technology integrations, client account fees, or even the cost of trading.

8. Who will be my point of contact if you are unavailable? It's not reasonable to expect anyone to be on call 24/7, and life happens. But it is reasonable to expect that a good professional will plan for such situations, and ensure that when they aren't available, their clients' needs are covered.

9. How frequently do you meet with your clients, and what should I expect during those meetings? What level of service will you get? Will you be charged extra fees if you want to schedule additional phone or video conference calls or in-person meetings with your advisor?

Although I've said this before, I will say it again: Do *not* take the easy way out by choosing the first professional you meet. Interview at least three before deciding on one.

As we reported at the beginning of Must-Know Fact 25, in a 2019 CNBC/Acorns study, only 17 percent of Americans reported working with a financial advisor, but it would be a mistake to conclude that because such a high percentage of individuals manage their own finances and investments that it must be a sound financial practice. While some self-directed investors may be long-term thinkers and possess all the necessary qualities for managing their own portfolios, others may learn the hard way that working with a professional would have been a better choice for them.

If you have a busy life or aren't comfortable with all the options out there for investing your money, consider developing a relationship with the financial expert who will best serve your needs. You can always change to self-management later, once you feel you are savvy enough about the financial world, so don't feel locked into any one choice.

ALLANISM

Knowledge is power. Listen, learn, and read about the stock market daily.

MUST-KNOW FACT 27

Robo-advisors are a solid option for investors who prefer to not pay higher fees to a live professional advisor.

Any sufficiently advanced technology
is equivalent to magic.
ARTHUR C. CLARKE, SCIENCE FICTION AUTHOR

———————

Now that you have read about the pros and cons of working with a financial advisor, let me give you one more option: investing your money with the assistance of a *robo-advisor*—an automated, but personalized, investment and wealth management solution.

The Birth of the Robo-Advisor

Robo-advisors were born, in a way, out of failure. The year was 2008. While the pains the financial industry suffered did not quite reach Depression-era levels, we experienced the subprime mortgage crisis and the Great Recession; unemployment hit 10 percent; and Lehman Brothers, a 158-year-old global financial services firm and a pillar of Wall Street that was viewed as "too big to fail," filed for bankruptcy and dissolved.

Around that time, a new way of competing with the Wall Street wolves was developing, and technology had finally advanced to the point it could be offered affordably and conveniently to the masses. Enter the robo-advisor.[57]

These digital financial planners were designed for individuals who wanted to put their money to work by automatically investing their funds and managing those investments just as a portfolio manager would—but without any direct input from a live person. The first robo-advisor firm was Betterment.com, which would later become the first robo-advisor to reach "unicorn" status—meaning it was a private startup with a pre-IPO valuation of more than $1 billion.[58] (If you ever happen to be on *Jeopardy!* and win with that answer, please let the millions of viewers know that you learned it from *The Wannabe Investor*!)

How Robo-Advisors Work

Individuals who use a robo-advisor have their money invested in certain assets based on their preferences and personal data—information they supply via a detailed online questionnaire. Their answers let the robo-advisor know their investment goals, their timelines, risk tolerance, current financial position, future financial needs, and more.

Based on the responses, the robo-advisor selects a portfolio of investments personalized to that investor, based on complex algorithms.

At this point, you will certainly be wondering what the pros and cons are of letting a robo-advisor manage your investments. And you should, because this is your money and you need to be as knowledgeable as possible about every choice you make.

Advantages of Using a Robo-Advisor

There are definitely advantages to using a robo-advisor:
- The setup is simple.
- You have access to your "advisor" twenty-four hours a day.

- The money management fees are lower than human advisors' fees.
- You can open an account with a robo-advisor firm with only a minimal starting investment.
- Each portfolio is created based on the individual financial needs and preferences of that investor.
- You can buy fractional shares of stock.
- The assets in a robo-advisor-managed portfolio will be automatically rebalanced (e.g., bought and sold) to stay aligned with your original risk level and asset allocation across classes.

Disadvantages of Using a Robo-Advisor

Now before you close this book and log on to www.betterment.com to set up an account, let's also consider a few of the disadvantages of using a robo-advisor.

- There is little, if any, direct guidance available to you from a live person. If you are going to need some emotional "handholding" when dealing with investing setbacks, you won't get it from a robo-advisor.
- You have limited options—the robo-advisor cannot comprehend complex investing strategies (at least not yet).
- Robo-advisors don't provide tax planning or estate planning services.
- Robo-advisors are limited based on the information you give them.
- The algorithms robo-advisors are built around are (so far) somewhat conservative. Any given portfolio designed by a robo-advisor may beat the market under some conditions and underperform it in others. But you're unlikely to get big outperformance at any point. The core rationale is to keep investors from fairly close to even with the market.

If you're interested in trying this hands-off way to invest, below is a list of some robo-advisors. Most have account minimums of $0 to $3000 with $500 being common, and most have a fee of a few dollars per month or an annual fee of 0.24% to 0.3% of assets under management. As always, do your research before choosing one.

- Acorns (www.acorns.com)
- Ally Invest Robo Portfolios (www.ally.com/invest/)
- Axos Managed Portfolios (www.axos.com)
- Betterment (www.betterment.com/)
- E-Trade (www.etrade.com)
- Sofi Investing (www.sofi.com)
- Vanguard Digital Advisor (investor.vanguard.com)
- Wealthfront (www.wealthfront.com)

To open your robo-advisor account, have the following information handy: your Social Security number, annual income, net worth, years of investing experience, investment goals, and risk tolerance level.

Hybrid Robo-Advisors

"You can't have your cake and eat it too." However, you sometimes *can*: when you work with a robo-advisor *and* a financial advisor. In fact, some people view the combination as the best of both worlds: it gives you professional advice from a real person but lets you manage your investments on a day-to-day basis with a robo-advisor. According to Donna Bristow, chief product officer of wealth management at Broadridge Financial Solutions, while a robo-advisor is a logical investment tool for someone who is testing the waters in investing or who is comfortable making their own decisions, consulting with a human advisor simultaneously provides the benefit of being able to actively manage emotions and tailor a portfolio to meet an investor's specific life-spanning needs.[59]

Regardless of how you work with a robo-advisor, I recommend you meet quarterly or annually with a fee-only financial advisor to be sure you are on track toward your financial goals.

ALLANISM

If you're curious about robo-advising, learning about it can be beneficial even if you don't end up using the service.

———————

MUST-KNOW FACT 28
Virtual trading lets you practice investing before putting your hard-earned money in the stock market.

Practice does not make perfect.
Only perfect practice makes perfect.
VINCE LOMBARDI, NFL COACH

————————

Just as you might (and should!) take skiing lessons before heading down a steep slope, before you put real money into the stock market, consider making a few practice investments with imaginary money through *virtual trading*, also known as *paper trading*.

Virtual trading allows people to trade securities using simulated accounts without risking any actual money. Virtual trading platforms provide users with real-time market data and allow them to "buy" and "sell" securities as if they were trading in the real market. The primary purpose of virtual trading is to help investors practice and develop their trading skills, test out different strategies, and gain confidence before investing their actual money in the stock market.

The Benefits of Virtual Trading

Virtual trading offers several benefits to newbie investors.

First, there is literally no risk. You can practice and develop your investing and trading skills with no possibility of wiping out your own hard-earned cash.

Second, even though you are investing with virtual money, these platforms give you real-time market data, allowing you to experience the true ups and downs of the market. You get a feel for how the market behaves over the course of a day, a week, a month, and so on.

Third, by experimenting with different strategies and techniques, you can gain confidence and improve your skills before investing for real. The practice may teach you more patience so that you don't make emotional decisions.

Lastly, virtual trading allows you to test different methods and techniques to see what works and what doesn't. You can figure out if there are business sectors you prefer or types of stocks that better suit your goals.

Disadvantages of Virtual Trading

While trading with virtual money can be a helpful way to learn about investing, it does have drawbacks. Even though you are watching the stock market rise and fall, paper trading doesn't reproduce the emotional and psychological factors involved in real investing. It's easy to make decisions in a calm, rational manner when nothing is at stake. Not so when actual money is on the line. Both fear of loss and fear of missing out can lead to irrational buying and selling choices.

Virtual trading platforms also don't factor in the impact of fees and taxes on your investment returns. In real investing, fees can eat into your returns significantly, especially if you trade frequently, and taxes will also have an impact. Believe me, these costs can make a big difference in the overall performance of your investments.

Trading simulators are just that—simulators. They aren't as reactive and don't necessarily shift quite as quickly as the real market, where timing can make a huge difference. These virtual trading platforms can also give you a false sense of confidence. Without real money at stake, you might make choices that wouldn't be advisable or fit your risk tolerance in a real-world investing scenario. Those risks might even pay off! But when you transition to real investing, you may find that your virtual strategies and stock-trading skills are not as effective as you thought they would be, which can lead to frustration and make you want to pull your money out of the market—unless you think long term.

Overall, virtual trading can be a great way to gain some practice, experience, and confidence. Just be aware of how putting your real money into real-world investments will affect your strategies and choices.

Getting Started with Virtual Trading

It's easy to get started with virtual trading:

Step 1: Choose a virtual trading platform. See the list below for some great options. (Alternately, you could track your virtual paper-trading portfolio on paper or via a simple spreadsheet program, but why go to that trouble when there are so many tools available that make it easier?)

Step 2: Create an account. You'll naturally have to provide your basic details, such as your name and email address, and you'll need to select a password. Some platforms may also require you to verify your identity with additional information.

Step 3: "Fund" your virtual account. Most virtual trading platforms provide users with accounts preloaded with a certain amount of virtual cash. Some do allow users to fund those accounts with additional pretend money if needed.

Step 4: Start picking and trading stocks. Once your account is set up, you can begin trading securities using virtual cash. The paper trading platform will provide real-time market data so that your transactions will give you the same results you'd get if you were trading in the real market.

Virtual Trading Platforms

There are numerous virtual trading platforms to choose from. Here are five from highly rated sources.

Interactive Brokers. This virtual simulator is called a paper trading account. You are given $1 million in virtual money. You must own and fund an account with Interactive Brokers to use their investing simulator.

TD Ameritrade. TD Ameritrade's virtual online trading environment, paperMoney, is built into the company's Thinkorswim trading platform. You are given $100,000 in virtual currency. If you are not a TD Ameritrade customer, you have sixty days to test the tool.

TradeStation. This simulated trading tool offers the full features of its real-life trading platform, including providing reports of your gains and losses. You choose the amount of virtual money you want. The platform is available only for TradeStation clients.

Webull. This stock trading simulator, Webull Paper Money, can help you determine when you are ready to begin your investment journey with real money. You can set your own account values, and you do not need to be a Webull customer to register for its virtual trading tool.

Investopedia. This simulator has many of the features listed above as well as a "learn" tab that provides information about the stocks themselves. Investopedia also has a cryptocurrency trading simulator.

There are other stock simulators as well, so do your homework and figure out which feels like the most user-friendly interface for you.

ALLANISM

Virtual trading is like playing Monopoly. Most people don't take it as seriously as they would investing their own hard-earned money.

MUST-KNOW FACT 29

There are emotional ways and logical ways to decide which investments to buy.

The trick is not to learn to trust your gut feelings,
but rather to discipline yourself to ignore them.
PETER LYNCH, INVESTOR AND AUTHOR

———————
————

At this point, you may be chomping at the bit to buy your first stock. But let's not get too hasty!

There's so much to know about investing. To this day, I find that the more I learn about investing, the more there is for me to learn. My plan is to never stop pursuing more knowledge on this topic, as it seems practically limitless. My hope is that you, too, will approach investing with a "thirst for knowledge" mindset. That will help keep you grounded as you're building your stock portfolio, and help you make better choices along the way. The last thing you want to do is treat stock-buying like a game of pin the tail on the donkey. Don't buy stocks randomly, or because they look like they are part of the "next big trend," or because you heard someone who sounded knowledgeable talk up a particular company.

When you see a stock you want to buy, first figure out your personal motivation for wanting to buy it. Is it one of the four stock-picking strategies described below? The first two strategies are far from analytical. The last two, however, are logical ways to determine if it's a good time to buy.

Buying Strategy 1: Based on FOMO (Fear of Missing Out)

While the acronym FOMO initially appeared in marketing literature in 2000,[60] the emotion behind it has been around forever. Just as some people impulsively buy things they don't need simply because they're on sale, or go to parties they don't want to attend because they worry they will regret their absence later, investors can be driven by similar fears to "buy now." If you see others jumping into a stock that "everyone" says is going "to the moon," it can be hard to resist joining the crowd. After all, who wants to be left behind while others are getting rich quick? This can be a particular temptation when it comes to the so-called "meme stocks" that surge because of blasts of social media attention. (The same applies to cryptocurrencies—and doubly so, because much less of their price action is driven by fundamentals and much more is driven by emotion.)

Granted, some stocks bought for less-than-rational reasons may have legitimate long-term upsides. Consider the youngish fintech companies Upstart (UPST) and Lemonade (LMND). Upstart is trying to disrupt the business of approving loans, an area that is overdue for an upgrade. Lemonade aims to do something similar in insurance, which is likewise ripe for a customer-friendly makeover. Both went public in 2020, and their stocks initially increased in value sharply due to emotion-driven trading. No doubt watching them rise lured in plenty of FOMO-feeling traders.

But when the upbeat emotions receded, the FOMO buying faded. The companies' results and outlooks in the short term were less stellar than investors hoped, and both stocks plunged. Anyone who bought Upstart as it was headed toward its peak above $330 a share probably wishes they had missed out; as of late 2023 shares are trading at less than $30. And more or less everyone who ever bought into Lemonade is looking at paper losses as I write this. After peaking at around $164 in February

2021, it's near its all-time low, below $12. And yet both of these companies have strong products and technology. It's not absurd to imagine them growing steadily over the long term, bid up gradually by investors who base their buying decisions on fundamentals, not FOMO.

That contrasts with what happened to AMC Entertainment Holdings (AMC) stock over the past few years. When the pandemic closed the doors of all movie theaters, the company—already in some difficulty before that, thanks to years of steady declines in box office sales—appeared on the brink of disappearing. Some millennials, driven both by nostalgia and by a desire to game the market and take advantage of the institutional short sellers who were betting heavily on the company's collapse, turned AMC into a meme stock. It worked. Others hopped on the bandwagon (much as they had when they drove the meteoric rise of GameStop if you're familiar with that case). However, AMC had fundamental financial troubles to deal with, and the stock plummeted again. Despite a few more short squeezes in the years that followed, AMC now trades for even less than it did on April 1, 2020, when fears of what the pandemic would do to the multiplex operator were perhaps at their sharpest.

Meme stocks are often highly popular among retail investors who spend time looking for tips on social media platforms such as Reddit, StockTwits, X (formerly known as Twitter), and Facebook. But just as you should not trust social media for medical advice, you should not trust it for stock advice. As we'll point out below, you should analyze stocks from either a fundamental standpoint, a technical standpoint, or both, to assess whether or not they are good investments and if the timing is right to buy them. If your fact-based, logical analysis indicates that it's the right stock and the right time to buy, then go for it! On the other hand, if you find that it is not the right time to buy, simply keep the stock on your watch list (which we'll talk about in Must-Know Fact 30) as one to re-examine in the future.

Buying Strategy 2: Based on Your Gut

Just as a stock buy based on FOMO is an emotional purchase, going with your gut is a gutsy way (pun entirely intended) to make an investment. If you do it, be sure you're not using money that you'll need anytime soon for a house payment or the electricity bill. Lots of people pick stocks based on their gut feelings—investing based on their familiarity with the services or products a company sells, and how they feel about them. In fact, my personal financial guru told me that his first stock purchase was based on a combination of FOMO and gut feelings!

Allan is a retired violinist who played for many years with the New York Philharmonic. Before landing that position, he freelanced. When he was twenty-two, one of his gigs was to play the Brahms Solo Violin Concerto at the Brooklyn Museum of Art. For that performance, he was paid $100 (the equivalent of about $1,100 today). Prior to the performance, a fellow musician mentioned to him that the orchestral conductor was a rich man. When Allan asked how he had acquired his wealth, his colleague said, "He owns many shares of Coca-Cola stock." Allan didn't drink Coca-Cola, and back then, he had no idea how to evaluate stocks. But he thought, *If this man got rich from Coca-Cola, then maybe I could, too.*

That day was a turning point for Allan, both for being appreciated as a fine musician (he would go on to have an amazing career) and for marking the beginning of his journey as a stock investor. The following day, he withdrew $1,000 from his savings account and invested in 10 shares of Coca-Cola, which was selling at about $100 a share. He bought this stock based merely on something he had heard secondhand about investing. Talk about a gutsy decision!

From the start, he believed in keeping his stocks for the long run, and because of that, his emotional decision has paid big dividends. As of October 25, 2022, the $1,000 or so that Allan invested in 10 shares of

Coca-Cola on May 1, 1958, was valued at a whopping $3.38 million! Coca-Cola shares split many times during those years. His original 10 shares grew to 11,520 shares, and by reinvesting his dividends, his stake grew over the years to about 59,100 shares. The beverage giant turned out to be a great pick for a young investor, even though he was following his gut when he bought it.

While I am not advocating buying stocks based on your gut instincts, I recognize that it can work, especially if you follow the most important tenet of investing: Think long term. (OMG! This must be the hundredth time I've written that in this book. I hope I've made my point.)

Buying Strategy 3: Fundamental Analysis

Though I've mostly relied on my own descriptions and experience thus far in the book, Kadi Arula of the financial news site Finbold offers such a good definition of *fundamental analysis* that paraphrasing it would only make it less clear. Arula writes:

> Fundamental analysis (FA) is a method that helps to determine whether an asset or a security is trading at a discount or its premium compared to its fair value. . . . The overall goal of fundamental analysis is to find and determine whether the asset is under or overvalued and to calculate its fair or intrinsic value.[61]

Fundamental analysis is a valuable concept for investors to learn—or at least learn enough *about*—so that you can understand the reports produced by Wall Street analysts and other professional market gurus. It begins with *quantitative analysis* of several factors, all of which are specific to each company:

- Financial statements

- Income statements
- Balance sheets
- Price-to-earnings ratio
- Dividends
- Other documents that describe the financial state of the company

Savvy investors often buy stocks or add to positions that they already own when fundamental analysis tells them a stock is undervalued.

Qualitative analysis takes fundamental analysis one step further by also looking at nonquantifiable elements, such as a company's brand name recognition, patents, and proprietary technology.

Fundamental analysis is such an important topic that investors can and do study it for years in an attempt to master the art. But even a basic grasp of it can give investors a big leg up. If this type of stock analysis speaks to you, I recommend you start by investing in a copy of Matt Krantz's *Fundamental Analysis for Dummies*.

Buying Strategy 4: Technical Analysis

While fundamental analysis assesses a company's strength, potential, and value, *technical analysis* assesses investment opportunities by looking at a stock's trading statistics, such as price movement and volume.

Analyzing a stock from a technical perspective involves studying its charts. I'm guessing that by now you've begun to dip your toes into the torrential river of stock information online and will have looked at the stock charts of at least a few companies you're interested in. Those line graphs plotting share prices may look almost random, and wild in their oscillations. Those who believe in the value of technical analysis will say that they are anything but random—that by watching for certain patterns, you can make reasonable predictions about what a stock will do next.

Traders—by which I mean people who buy and sell frequently (even daily) in an attempt to profit from short-term price moves—often use technical analysis to tell them when to buy and sell. I don't trade with that type of frequency, but I have found that technical analysis is a good tool to use in my efforts to determine if the timing is right to invest in a particular stock. One of my favorite books on technical analysis is Barbara Rockefeller's *Technical Analysis for Dummies*. If this style of assessing stocks appeals to you, it will be worth a read.

Whichever route you choose in the market, your best investment will be in knowledge. Studying how stocks behave on a deeper level and continually expanding your knowledge base should pay off many times over the years.

ALLANISM

Evaluate a stock from a fundamental or technical analysis standpoint rather than buying it just because you use the company's product or service.

———

MUST-KNOW FACT 30

Buying a stock requires planning; just as you plan other purchases, it is important to create a watch list for buying stocks.

Plans are nothing; planning is everything.
DWIGHT D. EISENHOWER, MILITARY OFFICER AND US PRESIDENT

———————

To invest, you must first decide which stocks to buy. There are many options available, and having so many choices can be daunting. One strategy to keep you focused on your investment goals is to create a stock "shopping list." Just like your list for grocery shopping, a list for stock shopping can help you get the things you want while avoiding impulse buys.

The goal with your stock shopping list is to identify stocks you are interested in buying before you're ready to lay out your hard-earned money. That way, you can track those potential investments, learn to recognize buying opportunities, and be ready to buy when a stock falls to an attractive price.

A stock shopping list, or *watch list*, helps you:

- **Stay organized and focused on your investment goals.** It can be overwhelming to try to keep track of even a fraction of the available stocks you could buy, especially when you are still learning the ropes.

162

- **Avoid making emotional decisions about which stocks to buy.** Even seasoned investors can get caught up in the excitement surrounding a "hot" stock. Investing based on emotions, however, can lead to poor decisions.
- **Recognize better buying opportunities when they appear.** Stock prices can quickly rise and fall. Tracking a stock's movements over time—and keeping up to date about the factors driving those movements—can give you more confidence to buy (or sell) at smarter times.

If you have a shopping list, you will very likely be more proactive about researching and evaluating potential stocks before you buy anything. And it will minimize the chance of making an impulse buy just because you heard a pundit talking about how that equity was ripe for the picking. If you're interested in a stock, put it on your list, and wait a bit. Do your own due diligence. If it looks like it's going to be a long-term winner, you can always buy it later.

Also, while it is good to listen to what the "experts" say about what to buy (and when to buy it), I highly recommend assessing the stocks on your watch list from a fundamental perspective, a technical perspective, or both. The best book I have found on this topic to date is A.Z Penn's *Technical and Fundamental Analysis for Beginners*. This book is a must-order for your library, especially as you create a shopping list, and certainly before you buy your first stock.

Criteria for a List-Worthy Stock

As you assess stocks for your watch list, here are some criteria to consider.

Competitive advantages: Does this company have a moat? As we covered in Must-Know Fact 16, businesses with sustainable competitive advantages that will allow them to maintain or grow their market shares over time tend to deliver better results to their investors.

Strong financials: A company's financials are a vital indicator of its potential as an investment. When assessing an organization's financials, review its revenue growth, profitability (or, if it's not profitable, whether it has a clear path to profitability), debt levels, and cash flow.

Good management: A company's leadership can have a big impact on its success. Look for companies with experienced and competent management teams. Learn what you can about those top executives' management philosophies; often, they will have been quite open about their priorities and plans for their company.

Positioning to benefit from trends: Consider what trends are having the biggest impact on the industry that the company operates within, and which trends look poised to impact it in the near future. Is the whole industry growing, stagnating, or declining? Are new technologies or products emerging that could disrupt the industry? Where is your prospective watch list stock relative to those trends: is it leading the charge, or about to get trampled by it?

Attractive valuation: Based on the fundamentals, is the stock trading at a fair price? Is it being overvalued? Or perhaps even undervalued? One way to gauge that is by looking at common valuation metrics such as the price-to-earnings ratio, the price-to-sales ratio, and the price/earnings-to-growth ratio (PEG ratio) to get an indication of whether the stock is a good value relative to both its peers and its historical valuations. Data about those metrics can be found at numerous sites online.

Different Types of Stock Shopping Lists

Different shopping trips call for different lists: just as you have a different list for the supermarket than you have for the mall, you'll want different lists curated for specific types of investments.

For instance, you might have individual lists for intriguing small-cap stocks, potential buys among companies that have recently gone public, value stocks you're researching, or growth stocks you think are over-priced but that you'd buy if their price dropped. Since *The Wannabe Investor's* focus is to assist you in building a foundation for your long-term investments, I would certainly propose that you create watch lists of both value stocks and growth stocks.

Having a stock shopping list is a smart strategy for all investors—from novices to seasoned stock pickers. To this day, I buy only stocks that have been on my shopping list first. By building your list around stocks that meet many (or all) of the criteria above, you can put yourself on the path to building an actual portfolio with the potential to generate significant returns over time.

ALLANISM

As a long-term investor, don't be distracted by the noise of the talking heads in the media.

———————

MUST-KNOW FACT 31
To invest in the stock market, you need to open a brokerage account.

Life is really simple, but we insist on making it complicated.
CONFUCIUS

———————

I distinctly remember the jumble of butterflies in my stomach the day I opened my first brokerage account. I soon learned that Allan was right—the process was no different than opening a checking or savings account, and there was nothing to be nervous about.

If you are among the roughly 40 percent of Americans who are not invested in the stock market at all, and one of your reasons is that you don't know where to begin when it comes to opening a brokerage account, you'll be able to cross that excuse off your list shortly, because I'm going to walk you step by step through the process.

Deciding on a Brokerage Account

A *brokerage account* is simply an account with a brokerage firm through which you can buy, hold, and sell stocks, bonds, mutual funds, and other securities. Just as a checking or savings account holds your money under the management of a bank, with a brokerage account, your investments are held under the custodianship of the broker. You and I—ordinary folks who are putting our own relatively small sums to work in the market—are considered to be *retail investors* (as opposed to large institutional investors).

There are three things you need to decide before you choose a brokerage account: your *what*, your *which*, and your *how long*.

What type(s) of account(s) do you want to open? If you are self-employed or a business owner, you may want to open a Roth IRA. If you worked for an organization that offered an employer-sponsored retirement plan such as a 401(k) or 403(b) and have since found employment elsewhere, you may also want to talk with a financial professional about opening a rollover IRA. This will allow you to "roll over" the funds you have in your former employer's plan to an IRA that's under your control, without losing the tax-deferred status of the assets in question. (Talk to an expert to make sure you perform rollovers correctly, or you may face penalties.)

Beyond those accounts, you'll also likely want a basic brokerage account. Tax-advantaged IRAs are great tools, but they limit the amount of money you can invest each year. In 2024, the cap is $7,000 ($8,000 for people age fifty and over). IRAs are also intended to be used strictly for retirement savings; taking money out early can lead to expensive penalties and taxes. So if you plan to put more than $7,000 in the market in some years, or are investing with goals other than retirement in mind, you'll certainly need a plain-Jane brokerage account.

In *which* types of assets do you intend to invest? While most brokers will facilitate trades of stocks, mutual funds, and ETFs, if you are thinking about trying other investment types, such as cryptocurrencies, make sure the brokerage firms you are considering support the trading of those particular assets. Just as an example, as of this writing, Merrill Edge doesn't give its clients the ability to trade directly in crypto, and it doesn't allow them to buy fractional shares of stock, mutual funds, or exchange-traded funds.

How long do you intend to hold the investments you buy? If you intend to actively trade stocks, be aware of the transaction fees that you might incur. While most brokerage firms no longer charge transaction fees for buying or selling stocks or ETFs online, that's not the case for all of them, so read the fine print.

Besides the *what*, *which*, and *how long* questions, consider minimums, commissions, and any other applicable fees. Most brokerage firms do not require you to deposit a minimum amount to open an account, but some do. And in addition to transaction fees, look at any commissions or other types of fees you may have to pay. Some fees will vary according to the size of your account. Again, read the fine print.

Finally, for investors who are just starting out, I strongly recommend choosing a brokerage firm that has a high rating for its customer support. Many online brokers have customer service representatives available 24/7 by phone, email, and online chat. Others are available 24/7 by phone. And some also offer in-person support at their brick-and-mortar branches. If you think you're likely to want after-hours support from time to time, check the brokerage's hours.

Quality Online Brokers

You have plenty of brokers to choose from, but here are a few that are known for their excellent customer service, zero-commission structures, lack of account minimums or transaction fees, and user-friendly trading platforms. In addition to larger full-service brokers, you may want to consider lower-cost options that allow the self-directed investor to access investment tools on their own, forgoing high-touch customer service in favor of saving money.

- Charles Schwab
- E-Trade
- Fidelity Investments

- Firstrade
- Interactive Brokers
- Merrill Edge
- Tastytrade
- TradeStation
- Vanguard

You will be in good hands with any of these online brokerage firms.

Opening a Brokerage Account

Now that you have an idea of what you should look for when choosing a brokerage account, let's explain how to open one.

Step 1: Choose a brokerage firm. While most firms have brick-and-mortar offices, if you are tech-savvy, you'll be able to manage most of your interactions using their online services. If you're not, however, you would be well advised to choose a firm that has an office located near you.

Step 2: Gather the necessary documents. What is required may vary by firm, but most will require you to supply a combination of the following: Social Security number or Tax Identification Number; government-issued identification, such as driver's license or passport; proof of address, such as a utility bill or lease agreement; and bank account information.

Step 3: Complete the application. The application will typically ask for your personal information, investment objectives, and trading experience. Answer these questions truthfully and accurately so that your broker will be better able to recommend appropriate investments and trading strategies for you.

Step 4: Fund your account. This is typically done either through a bank transfer, a wire transfer, or a check to the brokerage firm. Some firms also allow you to fund your account using a credit card or debit card. Be aware that bank transfers can take several days to clear. Debit card transactions (where allowed) may clear faster, but there may be surcharges.

Step 5: Start investing. Once your account is funded, you are ready to start investing. You can choose to buy individual stocks, bonds, mutual funds, or other securities, depending on what your broker offers. Remember: investing always carries some degree of risk, so it is important to do your research and invest wisely.

All told, up to the point where you have to start picking investments, this process is almost exactly the same as opening a regular bank account. Follow these steps, and in just a few days, you too can be a stock market investor!

ALLANISM

Opening a brokerage account is as simple as opening a checking account.

———

MUST-KNOW FACT 32
Concentration risk is when a single security makes up a significant percentage of your portfolio.

Investing is not nearly as difficult as it looks. Successful investing involves doing a few things right and avoiding serious mistakes.
JOHN C. BOGEL, FOUNDER OF VANGUARD

———————

So you've opened your brokerage account—yay, you! Now what? This is where the rubber hits the road! It's time to start buying. In this Must-Know Fact, I want to share two common pieces of practical investing advice and then test them out with a hypothetical portfolio—a little bit of our own virtual trading, you might say.

Two Pieces of Investing Advice for Beginners

Let me preface this advice with the reminder that everything takes time. It might take a while to reach "compliance" with these "rules"—and you might decide other "rules" are more important to you. With that said, here we go.

Buy at least ten stocks. After you determine how much money you have to invest, you may wonder how many stocks to buy with your money. Some experts recommend that your portfolio should have at least ten stocks. The Motley Fool recommends a minimum of twenty-five. CNBC anchor and *Mad Money* host Jim Cramer says that he's held as many as thirty to forty stocks. The experts, as you can see, disagree with one another. And many seasoned investors don't have hard and fast rules. About all we can say for certain is that they generally agree on the principle that diversification is a pretty smart idea.

My personal investing guru, Allan, prefers to hold ten to fifteen stocks, representing numerous different industries. That type of diversified portfolio, he explains, will reduce the risk that you might otherwise have if you invest your funds in fewer stocks and only in a few sectors.

This next piece of advice will help clarify why I say invest in a minimum of ten stocks (and again, it might take you time to get to that number).

Follow the 10 percent rule. The 10 percent rule says that you should allocate no more than 10 percent of your portfolio to a single investment when you're purchasing it. If you're holding more than ten individual stocks, of course, that percentage could be even lower.

Obviously, after you make investments, some of your picks will perform better than others. Your winners will come to represent more of your portfolio's value, your losers less of it. That's natural and desirable. But when you're making your original investments, it's not wise to put too many of your eggs in one (asset) basket.

Testing This Advice with a Hypothetical Portfolio

Let me give you a stock investing scenario with some specific picks to see how this advice works.

Let's imagine that you have funded your portfolio with $100,000 and plan to invest about $60,000 of it in individual stocks. Because you know the value of diversification, you decide to follow the 10 percent allocation guideline. You further decide to pick eleven companies—one from each of the eleven major business sectors (see Must-Know Fact 14)—and put about $5,500 into each one. And because you understand the power of long-term thinking in the market, you commit to yourself that you'll hold on to those shares for a minimum of ten years.

You've also determined some criteria for the companies that you'll consider. You will invest only in those that are a minimum of ten years old and have at least one durable competitive advantage (moat).

Now, even though you're keeping a lot of the things you've learned from *The Wannabe Investor* in mind with this plan, let's be clear: putting 60 percent of your investable assets directly into individual stocks is a moderate growth strategy (though it may be aggressive for a low-risk-tolerant investor). But we're assuming you've taken a long look in the mirror and decided you have the stomach to wait out the ups and downs.

At this writing it is late 2023, so let's set our starting point for this thought experiment back in January 2013. Then we can fast forward to see how your portfolio would have performed over a ten-year period.

Sector 1: Energy. **Stock**: Schlumberger (SLB): On the first trading day of 2013, Schlumberger's closing price was $71.40, so for $5,498, you could have bought 77 shares. On the first trading day of January 2023, it was valued at $51.50. Reality check: Your initial investment would have decreased to $3,966. Another reality check: Even with dividends reinvested, your stake would still be worth only $5,173. Your compound annual growth rate: −0.6%. (Yup, negative.)

Sector 2: Materials. **Stock**: Freeport-McMoRan (FCX): On the first trading day of 2013, Freeport-McMoRan's closing price was $35.17. A $5,487 investment would have bought you 156 shares. On the first trading day of 2023, Freeport-McMoRan closed at $37.92 per share. Your 156 shares would have been valued at $5,916. Factor in dividend reinvestment, and your stake would have grown to about $7,182. Your compound annual growth rate: 2.7%.

Sector 3: Industrials. **Stock**: Northrop Grumman (NOC): On the first trading day of 2013, Northrop Grumman closed at $68.17 per share. For

$5,522, you could have bought 81 shares. On the first trading day of 2023, Northrop Grumman closed at $540.33 per share. Your 81 shares would have been valued at $43,767. Factor in dividend reinvestment, and your stake would have grown to about $52,320. Your compound annual growth rate: 25.2%.

Sector 4: Consumer Discretionary. **Stock**: Starbucks (SBUX): On January 2, 2013, Starbucks closed at $55.37, so a $5,537 investment would have allowed you to buy 100 shares of this stock. On January 3, 2023, Starbucks' closing price was $100.83—and in the intervening time, it split 2-for-1. Your initial investment would have grown to about $20,170. With dividend reinvestment, your Starbucks stake would have been valued at $24,050. Your compound annual growth rate: 15.8%.

Sector 5: Consumer Staples. **Stock**: Coca-Cola (KO): On the first trading day of January 2013, Coca-Cola's closing price was $37.60. You would have been able to buy 146 shares for $5,490. On the first trading day of January 2023, those shares would have been valued at $62.95 apiece, giving you $9,191 in total. Had you reinvested your dividends, your stake would have been worth about $12,590. Your compound annual growth rate: 8.7%.

Sector 6: Health Care. **Stock**: Thermo Fisher Scientific (TMO): If you had invested $5,525 in Thermo Fisher on January 2, 2013, at its closing price of $65, it would have allowed you to buy 85 shares. On the first trading day of 2023, at Thermo Fisher's closing price of $553.18, your stake would have been worth just over $47,000. Had you reinvested your dividends, it would have been worth about $48,750. Your compound annual growth rate: 24.3%.

Sector 7: Financials. **Stock**: Interactive Brokers Group (IBKR): On the first trading day of 2013, Interactive Brokers Group's closing price was $13.89. A $5,500 investment would have allowed you to buy 396 shares of this stock. On the first trading day of 2023, Interactive Brokers Group's closing price was $71.38 per share, which means that your shares would have been valued at $28,266. Reinvest the dividends the company paid, and your result would have been about $29,230. Your compound annual growth rate: 18.2%.

Sector 8: Information Technology. **Stock**: Microsoft (MSFT): If you had bought 200 shares of Microsoft for $5,524 at the end of the first trading day of January 2013, when it had a closing price of $27.62 per share, and sold your shares on January 3, 2023, at their closing price of $239.78 per share, your initial investment would have grown to $47,920. And with dividend reinvestment, your holding would have been worth about $58,100. Your compound annual growth rate: 26.5%.

Sector 9: Communication Services. **Stock**: Verizon Communications (VZ): On January 2, 2013, Verizon closed at $44.27 a share. An allocation of $5,534 would have allowed you to buy 125 shares. On the first trading day of January 2023, it closed at $40.12 per share. But Verizon is a solid and steady dividend payer, so while the value of its shares sank by 7.3% over those years, if you had reinvested your dividends, you would have ended up with $8,094. Your compound annual growth rate: 3.9%.

Sector 10: Utilities. **Stock**: PG&E (PCG): If you had invested $5,515 in PG&E on the first trading day of 2013, you would have been able to buy 135 shares at the closing price of $40.85 per share. On the first trading day of 2023, PG&E closed at $15.68 per share. Your initial investment would have decreased to $2,117. Even factoring in dividend reinvestment, your stake would still only be worth $2,511. Your compound annual growth rate: −7.6%. (Another negative. Ouch.)

Sector 11: Real Estate. **Stock**: Simon Property Group (SPG): On the first trading day of 2013, Simon Property Group's closing price was $150.33. For $5,562, you would have picked up 37 shares of this stock. On the first trading day of January 2023, that real estate investment trust was valued at $117.54 per share. Your 37 shares would have been worth $4,349. Had you reinvested those payouts, your stake would have been worth $6,351. Your compound annual growth rate: 1.3%.

Now, you began with a total initial investment in individual stocks of $60,694. After a decade, your holdings (with dividends reinvested) would have had a value of $254,351, for a compound annual growth rate of 15.4%—impressively better than the S&P 500's typical long-term average of 10% or so. And overall, it amounts to 319% growth. Not bad!

It's also worth noting again that relatively small differences in compound annual growth rates can result in big differences in your returns over the long haul. That same sum, invested in an S&P 500 index fund over that same period, would have grown to $192,480—a 12.2% compound annual growth rate. (It was a better-than-average decade for the index.) But that seemingly minor 3.2% difference amounts to almost $62,000 after a decade—more than you invested in the first place.

Finally, let's point out that while putting 60% or so of your investable assets into individual stocks can be viewed as an aggressive strategy, this was not a super-aggressive set of stock picks. Only three of them were growth stocks: Starbucks, Thermo Fisher Scientific, and Interactive Brokers Group.

Seven were value stocks: Schlumberger, Freeport-McMoRan, Northrop Grumman, Coca-Cola, Verizon, PG&E, and Simon Property Group.

And Microsoft somewhat splits the difference between growth and value.

ALLANISM

Allocate no more than 5% to 10% of the assets in your portfolio to any one security.

———————

MUST-KNOW FACT 33

Dollar-cost averaging is a strategy in which you consistently invest the same amount in the same asset at regular intervals.

It is the greatest of all mistakes,
to do nothing because you can only do little.
SYDNEY SMITH, WRITER AND CLERIC

———————

As you read in the last Must-Know Fact, our hypothetical portfolio consisted of eleven stocks that we invested in all at the same time. That approach—buying the eleven stocks all at once—is called *lump-sum investing*.

While it may not be the right choice for you, I have been a proponent of lump-sum investing for more than three decades. Whether you receive an inheritance, win a large sum of money, or get an unexpected bonus at work, consider the lump-sum investment strategy. I favor it because the unexpected money is being put to work immediately.

It's more common, however, for most of us not to make one big lump-sum investment. We're earning and building up our nest egg gradually. So for many people, a different investing strategy may be more appropriate: dollar-cost averaging.

The term *dollar-cost averaging* was coined by Benjamin Graham in 1949 in *The Intelligent Investor,*[62] which many financial gurus regard as *the* book on investing. As Graham wrote:

Dollar-cost averaging means simply that the practitioner invests in common stocks the same number of dollars each month or each quarter. In this way, he buys more shares when the market is low than when it is high, and he is likely to end up with a satisfactory overall price for all his holdings.

Investors also call dollar-cost averaging the *constant dollar plan*. And actually, there are *two* constants in it:

1. The constant time intervals (e.g., weekly, monthly) over which you commit to buying the stocks or other assets.
2. The set amount of money that you commit to investing each time to buy those assets.

You could be using a dollar-cost averaging strategy without even realizing it. If you have a 401(k) account or something similar through your employer, you're making a preset contribution from each paycheck (whatever percentage you chose), which goes into the mutual funds and ETFs in your retirement account. When the market's down, your contribution buys you more shares of those funds. When it's up, you get fewer. That's dollar-cost averaging.

How Dollar-Cost Averaging Works

Here's a detailed example of how dollar-cost averaging works.

Let's say that beginning in January 2022, you decided that once a month, at the close of that month's first trading day, you were going to buy $1,000 worth of Microsoft stock. (Not an unusual pick—in the first quarter of 2019, it was the world's most widely held stock.[63]) For the sake of this example, we'll assume you wisely picked a brokerage that offers fractional share purchases.

You would have paid the following prices per share during 2022:

Jan 3: $334.75
Feb 1: $308.76
Mar 1: $294.95
Apr 1: $309.42
May 2: $284.47
Jun 1: $272.42
Jul 1: $259.58
Aug 1: $278.01
Sep 1: $281.92
Oct 1: $260.40
Nov 1: $228.17
Dec 1: $254.69

Add those per-share prices, and the total is $3,367.54.

Next, let's consider your *cost basis*, which in this case is defined as the average price you paid per share. (Cost basis can also be the total price you paid for an asset, so just be aware of which definition is in play—you should be able to tell by the context.) You can quickly figure out that number by dividing the total—$3,367.54—by 12. I'll spare you the calculator tapping: the average price paid per share was $280.63. and you ended up with 42.76 shares.

Now, in this exercise, you knew that you wanted to buy $12,000 worth of Microsoft in total. If you had purchased all of your shares on January 3, you would have paid $334.75 for each of them, and ended up with only 35.85 shares. By spreading out your purchases, you bought some shares at a lower price and some shares at a higher price, but you averaged out to a better price per share than you might otherwise have gotten. And you reduced the impact of the stock's short-term volatility on your investment.

"But wait!" I can hear some of you saying. "Wouldn't I have been even smarter to hold on until the price dropped even lower—like to the $228.17 it was on November 1?"

Sure, in theory. If you had a crystal ball to tell you when the low point of 2022's tech sector tumble was going to be, and where the low point of Microsoft's trough was going to be. But nobody has a working crystal ball, and trying to invest as if we do—in other words, attempting to *time the market*—is a recipe for disappointment.

Imagine if you had watched Microsoft's stuttering slide over that year and told yourself, "I'll wait to buy when it goes below $200." It never got that low. You'd never have bought at all, and you'd have missed out on Microsoft's nice rebound.

Now that you see what dollar-cost averaging is, it's your turn to do the same exercise with Alphabet (GOOG), which was the world's second-most widely held stock in the first quarter of 2019.

Here's how:

Step 1: Go to www.finance.yahoo.com.

Step 2: Enter GOOG in the Yahoo!Finance search bar.

Step 3: From the menu, click on Historical Data.

Step 4: Pick a year and find the price that GOOG closed at on the first trading days of those twelve months.

Step 5: Total those twelve stock prices.

Step 6: Divide the total by 12 and you'll have your cost basis (the average price you paid) for those GOOG shares.

Lump-Sum versus Dollar-Cost Averaging

You can probably already see some of the advantages of dollar-cost averaging:

- It adds discipline to your investing plan by committing you to invest the same amount in a given asset or set of assets each period.
- It safeguards you from putting off investing for the future until the "ideal" time.

- It takes your emotions out of the equation. Whether a stock you like is at its all-time high or has dipped to a five-year low, your autopilot investment strategy doesn't flinch. And that's important, because the fear of making the wrong move can be paralyzing.
- It's a solid alternative to lump-sum investing.

The benefits of dollar-cost averaging might lead you to conclude that lump-sum investing is a bad idea. It's not—when done smartly.

A study from Northwestern Mutual reports that historically a lump-sum investment approach would have produced higher returns than a dollar-cost average strategy.[64] Why? Because more of your money gets into the market sooner. And the longer the time frame, the greater the opportunity cost (in other words, the more lump-sum investing outpaces dollar-cost averaging). The study reports that on rolling ten-year returns on $1 million:

- Assuming a 100 percent *stock* portfolio, the return on lump-sum outperformed dollar-cost averaging 75 percent of the time.
- Assuming a 100 percent *bond* portfolio, the return on lump-sum outperformed dollar-cost averaging 90 percent of the time.

But there are a few things worth noting here. First, while lump-sum investing does often outperform dollar-cost averaging, that's not an absolute and any difference may be minor; certainly, either approach is better than doing nothing and losing your buying power to inflation. Second, as noted earlier, most of us don't have beaucoup bucks lying around just waiting to be dropped in the market. Finally, if you are a more conservative investor, if your risk tolerance is lower, you may be more comfortable with spreading your buys over time—and if that keeps you in the market, a dollar-cost averaging approach is worth it.

Essentially, there's no definitive answer to the question of which strategy is better. The choice is up to you and should be made based on your personal situation. But I would suggest that rather than holding your breath until you receive a windfall, you take control of your financial future by making investing a habit now—and dollar-cost averaging is an easy way to get started.

ALLANISM

Don't buy more than you can afford.

———————
————

MUST-KNOW FACT 34
The Dogs of the Dow strategy involves buying annually the ten Dow stocks with the highest dividend yields and holding them for a calendar year.

The wisest rule in investment is: When others are selling, buy.
When others are buying, sell. Usually, of course, we do the opposite.
JONATHAN SACKS, ORTHODOX RABBI AND AUTHOR

———————

Let's say you want to invest on your own, yet you don't have the time or resources to extensively research and analyze stocks. If that's the case, can I ever relate! That's exactly how I felt early in my stock-picking period. While in principle I trusted the strategies and tactics I'd learned, as a wannabe, I was still scared to actually bite the bullet and start buying.

That's when Allan introduced me to the "Dogs of the Dow" strategy. Not only is it reliable but using this strategy to set up your portfolio (or a portion of it) will take you literally one hour a year—if that long!

The Dogs of the Dow Strategy

As you'll remember from our discussion of index funds, the Dow Jones Industrial Average (DJIA, or the Dow) is made up of thirty large-cap and mega-cap companies across a variety of industries—all of them viewed as high-quality businesses. In fact, almost by definition, a stock in the DJIA is a blue-chip stock. The Dogs of the Dow strategy is an investment approach that involves buying equal dollar amounts of the ten stocks in the Dow 30 that have the highest dividend yields on the first business day of the year and then holding them for the entire calendar year.

Dividend yield is a ratio (expressed as a percentage) calculated by dividing the dividends paid by the current stock price. For example, if a company is paying $2 per share in annual dividends and its stock price is $16 per share, the dividend yield is $2/$16, or 12.5%. Companies with the highest dividend yield are typically in the downside of their business cycle, and their share price has fallen as a result. This pushes the dividend yield up.

To fully benefit from this strategy, it is essential that the ten Dogs be purchased on the first business day of the year and held until the last business day of the year. Then on the first business day of the following year, the stocks are sold, and the strategy is repeated with the ten *new* Dogs. Of course, if some of the Dogs repeat from one year to the next, there's no need to sell and rebuy the same shares; simply adjust your holdings to the right proportion (an equal dollar amount in each of the ten).

This strategy gets its name from the idea that these high-yielding stocks are "dogs"—in other words, they've recently been lagging the market as a whole. But the theory is that they have been bid down excessively and that as they recover from their laggard positions, they're likely to outperform the other stocks in the Dow in the coming year. The strategy follows the principle of *contrarian investing*, which means doing the opposite of what other investors may be doing, such as buying stocks that have fallen out of favor due to negative news or market conditions. As a result of their lower prices, these stocks may have high dividend yields. The idea is that investors can profit from the combination of the relative strength of Dow stocks and the opportunity to buy undervalued components using high dividend yields as a proxy for low valuation.

The Dogs of the Dow strategy gained popularity after Michael O'Higgins published his book *Beating the Dow* in 1991. (If you happen to have picked up a few other investing books before coming to *The Wannabe Investor,* you might have read John Slatter's 1991 book, *Safe Investing: How to Make Money Without Losing Your Shirt*; if so, you may have noticed that the Dogs of the Dow concept was also mentioned there. O'Higgins, however, seems to get most of the credit for popularizing it.)

Table 9 shows the positions of the ten Dogs of the Dow as of December 29, 2023, so you can see the current Dogs and Small Dogs.

Table 9. The 2024 Dogs of the Dow ranked by dividend yield

Company	Price	Dividend Yield	Small Dog?
Walgreens (WBA)	26.11	7.35%	Yes
Verizon (VZ)	37.70	7.06%	Yes
3M (MMM)	109.32	5.49%	No
Dow (DOW)	54.84	5.11%	Yes
IBM (IBM)	163.55	4.06%	No
Chevron (CVX)	149.16	4.05%	No
Coca-Cola (KO)	58.93	3.12%	Yes
Amgen (AMGN)	288.02	3.12%	No
Cisco Systems (CSCO)	50.52	3.09%	Yes
Johnson & Johnson (JNJ)	156.74	3.04%	No

Does the Dogs of the Dow strategy work?

This investing strategy sounds reasonable, but does it beat the market? It depends on the years in which you use this strategy.

For example, if you look at the years from 2000 through 2007, which included the dot-com bust and the general recovery that followed (though not so much for tech stocks), the Dogs returned 3.38%, beating the Dow, which returned 2.56%.

From 2013 to 2023, the Dogs had an average annual return of 10.02%, while the entire Dow index delivered an average annual return of 11.48%.[65]

From 1973 to 2016, the Dogs of the Dow strategy returned an average of 10.5% annually, compared to 7.8% for the DJIA and 9.7% for the S&P 500.

And if you look at the twenty-year period ending December 2022, you will find the remarkable result that the Dogs delivered a 10.8% annualized total return, and the full DJIA delivered . . . a 10.8% annualized total return.[66] Exactly the same result!

As you can see, the question of gauging performance really comes down to when you start and stop the clock.

In addition to the "Dow 10" strategy (which by now you can guess means buying the ten Dow stocks that pay the highest dividend yields), there are two other Dogs of the Dow strategies, called the *Small* Dogs of the Dow.

The first Small Dog variation comes from O'Higgins as well and is sometimes called the "Flying Five." In this strategy, you again begin with the ten Dow stocks with the highest dividend yield, and you invest in the five with the lowest price. Over the twenty-year period just mentioned (ending December 2022), the Small Dogs had annualized total returns of 12.6%, outperforming both the Dogs and the overall Dow.

The second Small Dog variation is called the "Dow 4" strategy. It takes the same approach as the Flying Five, but as you may have guessed from its name, of the ten Dogs, you invest in the four with the lowest share price.

Table 10 compares the returns of the Dogs of the Dow and the Small Dogs of the Dow (five), to the Dow Jones Industrials and other indexes from 2015 through 2019. Over this time, both the Dogs and the Small Dogs outperformed the DJIA. Can you guess what the differentiating factor was? Dividends!

Table 10. Performance of Dow, Dogs, and Small Dogs 2015 through 2019

Investment	Symbol	2015	2016	2017	2018	2019
Dogs of the Dow	-	2.60%	20.80%	23.70%	0.00%	19.70%
Small Dogs of the Dow	-	10.30%	14.30%	12.80%	0.80%	9.70%
Dogs of the Dow X	-	8.10%	23.90%	23.80%	5.10%	17.30%
Small Dogs of the Dow X	-	14.30%	13.40%	20.50%	14.30%	9.20%
Dow Jones Industrials	-	0.20%	16.50%	28.10%	-3.50%	25.30%
S&P 500	-	1.40%	12.00%	21.80%	-4.40%	31.50%
Fidelity Magellan	FMAGX	4.10%	5.20%	26.50%	-5.60%	31.20%
Vanguard Index 500	VFINX	1.30%	11.80%	21.70%	-4.50%	31.30%

Note 1: All total returns are calculated using reinvested dividends.
Note 2: The effects of commissions/loads are not included.
Note 3: All data is believed to be from reliable sources.
Note 4: Past performance is in no way a guarantee of future results.
Note 5: The above listed mutual funds were selected for comparison due to the fact that they are among the largest U.S. domestic growth equity funds.
Table courtesy of Dogs of the Dow (https://www.dogsofthedow.com/dogyrs.htm).

Tables 11 and 12 show us how the Dogs of the Dow performed in 2022. [67] The Dogs ended the year with a −1.8% total return. That might look like chopped liver—until you see that the Dow Jones Industrial Average had a −8.4% return; even worse, the Small Dogs' total return was −21.0%!

Table 11. Dogs of the Dow 2022 performance

Company The Dogs of the Dow are listed in bold.		Price 12-30-21	Yield 12-30-21	Price 12-30-22	Yield 12-30-22	Change *Note 1
DOW	**Dow**	**56.72**	**4.94%**	**50.39**	**5.56%**	**-11.20%**
VZ	**Verizon**	**51.96**	**4.93%**	**39.49**	**6.62%**	**-24.20%**
IBM	**IBM**	**133.66**	**4.91%**	**140.89**	**4.68%**	**5.40%**
CVX	**Chevron**	**117.35**	**4.57%**	**179.49**	**3.16%**	**53.00%**
WBA	**Walgreens**	**52.16**	**3.66%**	**37.36**	**5.14%**	**-28.40%**
MRK	**Merck**	**76.64**	**3.60%**	**110.95**	**2.63%**	**44.80%**
AMGN	**Amgen**	**224.97**	**3.45%**	**262.64**	**3.24%**	**16.70%**
MMM	**3M**	**177.63**	**3.33%**	**119.92**	**4.97%**	**-32.50%**
KO	**Coca-Cola**	**59.21**	**2.84%**	**63.61**	**2.77%**	**7.40%**
INTC	**Intel**	**51.50**	**2.70%**	**26.43**	**5.52%**	**-48.70%**
JPM	JP Morgan Chase	158.35	2.53%	134.10	2.98%	-15.30%
JNJ	Johnson & Johnson	171.07	2.48%	176.65	2.56%	3.30%
CSCO	Cisco	63.37	2.34%	47.64	3.19%	-24.80%
TRV	Travelers	156.43	2.25%	187.49	1.98%	19.90%
CAT	Caterpillar	206.74	2.15%	239.56	2.00%	15.90%
PG	Procter & Gamble	163.58	2.13%	151.56	2.41%	-7.30%
GS	Goldman Sachs	382.55	2.09%	343.38	2.91%	-10.20%
MCD	McDonald's	268.07	2.06%	263.53	2.31%	-1.70%
HON	Honeywell	208.51	1.88%	214.30	1.92%	2.80%
HD	Home Depot	415.01	1.59%	315.86	2.41%	-23.90%
WMT	Walmart	144.69	1.52%	141.79	1.58%	-2.00%
UNH	UnitedHealth	502.14	1.16%	530.18	1.24%	5.60%
AXP	American Express	163.60	1.05%	147.75	1.41%	-9.70%
MSFT	Microsoft	336.32	0.74%	239.82	1.13%	-28.70%
NKE	Nike	166.67	0.73%	117.01	1.16%	-29.80%
V	Visa	216.71	0.69%	207.76	0.87%	-4.10%
AAPL	Apple	177.57	0.50%	129.93	0.71%	-26.80%
BA	Boeing	201.32	0.00%	190.49	0.00%	-5.40%
CRM	Salesforce	254.13	0.00%	132.59	0.00%	-47.80%
DIS	Disney	154.89	0.00%	86.88	0.00%	-43.90%

Table 12. Dogs of the Dow 2022 performance, compared

Index	Description	Price 12/31/2021	Yield 12/31/2021	Price 12/30/2022	Yield 12/30/2022	Change *Note 1
Dogs of the Dow	10 highest yielding Dow stocks on 12/31/21	-	3.89%	-	4.43%	-1.80%
Small Dogs	5 lowest priced Dogs on 12/31/21	-	3.81%	-	5.12%	- 21.00%
Dow 30	30 Dow stocks on 12/31/21	-	2.23%	-	2.57%	-8.40%
DJIA	Dow Jones Industrial Index	36,338.30	2.23%	33,147.25	2.57%	-8.80%

Note 1: YTD % change figures do not include for dividends, commissions, or taxes.

Note 2: Prices as of 12/31/21 are revised for subsequent price adjustments (e.g. stock splits) which occur during the following year. For a list of the Dogs of the Dow with their unadjusted 12/31/21 prices, see the 2022 Dogs of the Dow.

Tables courtesy of Dogs of the Dow (https://www.dogsofthedow.com/dogs2022p.htm).

Six Steps for Investing in the Dogs of the Dow

By now, you may be chomping at the bit to put your money to work in the Dogs of the Dow. And as I said, it won't take you much time or effort to do the research. Determining which Dow stocks have the highest dividend yields (or had them last year) can be done online.

Before you do, however, I urge you to take a second look at Table 10 above. While the average return for the Dogs of the Dow was 13.3% and the average return for the Small Dogs of the Dow was 9.58%, these returns are over a five-year period. Remember, the name of the game in investing is to *think long term*!

With that word of advice, here is a step-by-step approach for a new investor to invest in the Dogs of the Dow strategy:

Step 1: Open a brokerage account. If you've already opened an account with a reputable broker as discussed earlier in this book, continue. If you have not yet done so, see Must-Know Fact 31 for guidance.

Step 2: Fund your account. Fund your brokerage account with the money you plan to invest by transferring the money from your bank account or depositing a check.

Step 3: Start buying. Buy equal dollar amounts of the ten highest-dividend-yielding stocks on the Dow Jones Industrial Average list (or the four or five Small Dogs, if that's your preferred strategy). You can find this information online or through your broker. (To make it even easier, you could subscribe to the free Dogs of the Dow Newsletter at www.dogsofthedow.com.) Ideally, you would begin this investment strategy on the first trading day of the year.

Step 4: Hold the stocks for one full calendar year. An essential criterion of being successful with this strategy is to buy the ten stocks on the first business day of the year and hold the stocks for an entire year. If you hold them for at least a year, it will put your investment into the long-term capital gains category, which can lower your tax burden when you sell. (We'll discuss sales and capital gains in Must-Know Fact 37.)

Step 5: Review and rebalance. At the end of the year, review your portfolio. Then on the first business day of the following year, rebalance your Dogs of the Dow portfolio by selling or buying as needed to ensure that you are still invested in the ten highest-dividend-yielding stocks in the DJIA. That is, make sure your portfolio has equal proportions of the ten *new* Dogs. (We'll talk about the implications of selling stock in Must-Know Facts 37 and 38.)

Step 6: Repeat the process each year. Once you have rebalanced your portfolio, repeat the process by holding the stocks for another year and then reviewing and rebalancing at the end of *that* year. Repeat each year!

Overall, the Dogs of the Dow strategy is a simple, straightforward approach to investing in blue-chip companies with high dividend yields. However, while it's a solid strategy, it is somewhat conservative. Most the Dow stocks are mature companies more likely to reward investors with regular dividends than with rapid growth. So while you are choosing the Dogs in anticipation of an improving stock price, you're unlikely to see the soaring returns of an Nvidia with these stocks. As with any investment strategy, it's important to do your research and understand the pros and cons involved before investing.

ALLANISM

Past performance of a stock does not guarantee its future results.

———————

MUST-KNOW FACT 35
You can buy and sell a stock at its existing price, or you can set up an automated order based on predefined parameters.

A great business at a fair price is superior to a fair business at a great price.
CHARLIE MUNGER, FORMER VICE CHAIRMAN OF BERKSHIRE HATHAWAY

———————

You're ready. It's time. So, let's walk through the process of how to place a trade. As we start, you will no doubt feel as though most everything we're going over is so obvious and intuitive that there's no point in finishing this Must-Know Fact, but I suspect that you'll come across a thing or two that makes this short section worth your time. First, we'll go step by step through the simplest transaction process, then we'll cover some terminology related to more complex parameters that you can set to make automated transactions.

Steps to Make a Purchase

Every brokerage's app and website will have their own unique look. But what we're going to cover should be more or less universal. You might have to look for slightly different language, you might see tabs rather than icons, and the steps might be in a slightly different order—but you'll get the idea.

To make things fun, let's buy $1,000 of Apple stock.

Step 1: Log in to your brokerage account by keying in your username and password.

Step 2: Click on the *Trade* icon, which will (no surprise) take you to the page where you will be able to place a trade. (Instead of "Trade" the label might be "Transact" and instead of an icon, it may be on a menu. Poke around—you'll find it.)

Step 3: You will likely see a field with a dropdown menu of choices of different asset classes available. Choose *Stocks*, since we're buying Apple.

Step 4: If you have more than one account with your brokerage firm, select the one from which you would like the money to be withdrawn to buy the Apple shares.

Step 5: In the appropriate field, enter the ticker symbol of the stock you would like to buy. Since we're buying Apple stock, you would type in AAPL. *Be sure you have the correct symbol.* (It's not impossible to mistake one company's ticker for another. Before Twitter IPOed back in 2013, some confused traders infamously bought up shares of the business with the symbol TWTRQ, which it turns out was not the social media company but bankrupt consumer electronics retailer Tweeter Home Entertainment Group. Oops!)

Step 6: In the "Action" section, you'll have the choice of *Buy* or *Sell*. Since you are making a purchase, select *Buy*.

Step 7: In the "Quantity" section, enter the number of shares you want to buy. Since you want to buy $1,000 of AAPL, if its price that day is $200 per share, you would buy 5 shares.

Step 8: In the "Order Type" field, choose *Market Order*, which indicates you want to buy or sell *now*, at whatever the current price is. (We'll discuss other choices shortly.)

Step 9: In the "Time in Force" field, choose *Day*.

Step 10: In the "Trade Type" field, choose *Cash*.

Step 11: Before you place the trade, choose *Preview* to confirm that the details of the purchase order you've prepared are correct.

Step 12: If the specifics in the preview section are correct, place your order! You will receive a confirmation email when it is complete.

Congratulations! You're not a wannabe anymore—you're an investor. You can see how the process for placing a sell would be similar—the main difference being you choose *Sell* rather than *Buy* in Step 6. But since we just got you *in* the market, let's set aside the detailed steps for selling. We're gonna think long term, right?

Other Ways to Buy and Sell Stocks

It might surprise you, but there's more than one way to buy or sell stocks. And as you get more experience, you may want to use some of these approaches.

The simplest transaction is a *Market Order*, which means you want to buy or sell *now*, at whatever the current price is. That's what we just did with our Apple purchase.

A *Limit Order* sets either the maximum price at which you are willing to buy, or the minimum price at which you will sell. For example, if you want to buy Apple but believe it is going to drop from the $200 per share price, you could try to get it for a lower price by creating a *Buy Limit Order* to buy AAPL for $165. If that price becomes available during the time frame for which you have set the order, your trade will automatically be executed. But if Apple's stock price never gets that low during the time frame, your order to buy will not be filled—and you'll miss out on whatever gains Apple shares produce.

On the other side of the coin, a *Sell Limit Order* sets a line that you hope the stock will cross heading upward. If you already owned Apple stock and would be ready to consider your investment a win if it rose to $230 a share, you could set that as your sell limit order. When Apple hits that price, whether you are paying any attention to the market that day or not, your sale will be executed.

There is also something called a *Stop Loss Order*, and it's exactly what it sounds like. If you own shares of a company that you fear might plunge in value, you can set a *floor*—a price below which you are not willing to hold on in hopes of a recovery—that is, the point at which you want to *stop* your *losses*. If the stock in question drops below the order's level, your shares will automatically be sold at the best available price after that.

And just to get deep into the weeds, there's an order type called a *Trailing Stop Order*. A trailing stop order doesn't set a specific price at which you want to sell but rather a *price action* after which you want to sell. So, for example, you could say "Sell my shares of Apple if they fall by 10% from their peak" or "Sell my shares of Apple if they fall by $35 from their peak." The actual point at which that order would go into effect will depend on the stock's performance.

While you may have the option of having the orders remain in place for a single day's trading session, in many instances you can choose *Good until Canceled*, which means your order will remain active until you cancel it. Others (depending on your broker) might expire after a set period, such as ninety days. That information appears in the field labeled "Time in Force" (or something similar).

There are other buy-sell options beyond these, but you're unlikely to need to worry about most of them for quite some time, if ever.

ALLANISM

**A stock doesn't know you own it;
it doesn't move according to your wishes.**

MUST-KNOW FACT 36

Your monthly brokerage statement provides your account's performance since the last statement period as well as the total value of your portfolio.

Keep going, and don't worry about your speed.
You're making progress, even if it doesn't seem like it.
LORI DESCHENE, AUTHOR AND FOUNDER OF TINY BUDDHA

When you transition from wannabe investor to actual investor, you will start to receive regular reports on your investments: brokerage account statements. Besides receiving a monthly document that provides an overview of your account values, you will also be sent an annual document at the end of the calendar year.

Before writing this section, I asked several individuals who invested in the market if they knew how to read their monthly statements. You may be as stunned as I was by their responses:

- "When I get my statement, I put it in a drawer—unopened, I am embarrassed to add!"
- "I think so. Sort of."
- "Not only do I not know how to read those statements—I have no clue what my investment advisor is talking about during our annual meeting."
- "I leave what my portfolio earns up to my financial advisor."

Hard to believe, isn't it? Think about it: These individuals have worked so hard to earn money to invest and now leave the growth of their funds to chance or, worse yet, to a stranger? Talk about blind faith . . . and, I hope, a decision you will not make yourself.

Perhaps if they'd taken the time to learn what to look for when reading their brokerage statement, they would have been more comfortable with the numbers and their responses may have been different. Simply knowing what to look for makes the statement feel much less intimidating, so let's go over the basics . . .

Pro tip: If you are receiving paper rather than electronic statements, I recommend you dedicate a three-ring notebook to these statements. I can tell you firsthand that it is a terrific way to stay organized and have easy access to them.

There are ten main areas on your statement for you to review. As with our earlier discussion of trading platforms, the terminology or location of information might vary slightly, but all statements should contain these elements in some form.

1. The statement beginning and end date. This is exactly what it sounds like. A brokerage statement, like any other financial statement, ends the period on the last business day of the month. An annual brokerage statement ends its period on the last business day of the year. You will typically find that date listed in the top right corner of your statement.

2. Your account number. The next piece of information to look for is your account number(s) and your name and address. Whenever you have a change of address, make certain you update your account and that your statement accurately reflects the change.

3. Your financial expert's contact information. If you have chosen to work with an investment expert, that person's contact information will be displayed so you have easy access for questions. If you have decided to manage your own brokerage account, you will find both a website address and a customer service toll-free number.

4. The clearing firm. A *clearing firm* serves as a bridge between broker-dealers and investors in managing transactions. While there are many clearing firms, a few with names you may recognize are Charles Schwab, Bank of New York, BNY Mellon's Pershing, and Fidelity National Financial Services LLC. (Note that this information may be in the fine print at the end of your statement.)

5. Your account summary. Usually in large type right up front you will see the total account value. Then you will see:

- The total account value at the beginning of the period
- A summary of additions (deposits, exchanges in), subtractions (withdrawals, exchanges out, transaction costs, fees, charges), and transfers between accounts
- The change in value from period beginning to period end
- The total account value at the end of the period

You may also see a note showing any interest that your account has accrued and a list of the top holdings in your account along with the percentage of each holding.

If you see that the total account value on this statement is less than it was on your last statement, remember the most important thing when investing: *think long term*!

6. Holdings. Here you will see a list of all your holdings, including stocks, bonds, ETFs, mutual funds, and so on, as well as your cash account (sometimes called your core account). For each holding, you will see (if applicable):

- The beginning and ending monthly market values
- The number of units held and the period-end price per unit
- Your cost basis
- Your net gain/loss (unrealized) (Unrealized means you have not actually sold, so there is no real gain or loss yet—any movement is just on paper.)

7. Activity. In this section you will find the transaction details behind all the earlier summary information, including any trades you have made (or that your investment broker has made on your behalf). You are likely to see:

- Securities you have bought and sold, including each trans-action with its date, number of units, and the price
- Dividends, interest, and other income you may have received along with the related transaction details
- Withdrawals or transfers you've made, including the date, the amount, and a description of where it went (e.g., to a bank account)
- Core fund activity, such as movement of funds into and out of your cash account

Be sure to compare the activity in this list to the trade confirmations you received during the statement period. They should match.

8. Fees. Your statement may have a section that lists any charges assessed for the month, or these fees may be listed in the transaction data. Transactional costs may include a stock trading commission, a brokerage fee, a management or advisory fee, a sales load if you own mutual funds, an expense ratio (which is an annual fee charged by mutual funds and ETFs). If you do not understand one or more of these fees, it is important that you ask the person with whom you have a financial relationship to explain it to you. If you are managing your own brokerage account, you should call the help center desk of the brokerage firm that holds your account. Just as you audit your checking account fees (you do, don't you?), be sure to audit the brokerage-related costs you are incurring.

9. Margins. If you sold a stock and then used that money to purchase another stock before the funds settled (in other words, before the transfer of funds from buyer to seller was complete), you bought *on margin*. Essentially you took a very short-term loan and were charged interest for it. You may see a separate section for margins.

10. Disclosures and definitions. It's easy for investors to overlook this section, but it's worth a read, as it explains fees and defines key terms.

See, I told you that reading a brokerage statement wasn't difficult. You simply have to know what you're looking for!

ALLANISM

When your stocks go up in price,
you think you're a genius for choosing them.
When they fall, you are humbled.

———

MUST-KNOW FACT 37
The length of time you hold an investment affects the tax rate you pay when selling it.

It takes a lot of time to be a genius;
you have to sit around so much doing nothing . . .
GERTRUDE STEIN, WRITER AND ART COLLECTOR

———————
———————

If I've given you one takeaway from this book, I hope it is this: Invest for the long term! My primary reason for that advice is the growth you can experience with dividends, compounding, and time in the market. But there is one other practical reason: taxes. Uncle Sam is also a fan of investing for the long term, so much so that he will cut you a break on your taxes if you refrain from short-term investing. Any discussion of investing would be incomplete without a mention of capital gains taxes, so here we go.

The term *capital gain* refers to the increase in the value of an asset when it is sold. When you sell a stock for more than you paid for it, the profit is your capital gain. The same applies to the profits on mutual funds, ETFs, crypto, and so on—they are all assets. (Likewise, you can have a *capital loss* if the value decreases.)

Just as you owe income taxes on the money you earn by working, you owe capital gains tax on the profits you accrue by investing. How *much* you owe is based on two criteria: the length of time you have held the asset in question, and your household's taxable income.

LONG-TERM CAPITAL GAINS TAX

If you've held your investment more than a year, it is considered a *long-term holding* and you pay long-term capital gains tax rates. Table 13 displays long-term capital gains tax rates by taxable income for tax years beginning in 2024.[68]

Table 13. Long-term capital gains tax rates by taxable income for tax years beginning in 2024

Filing status	0% Rate	15% Rate	20% Rate
Married filing jointly	Up to $94,050	$94,051 to $583,750	Over $583,750
Married filing separately	Up to $47,025	$47,026 to $291,850	Over $291,850
Head of household	Up to $63,000	$63,001 to $551,350	Over $551,350
Single	Up to $47,025	$47,026 to $518,900	Over $518,900
Estates and trusts	Up to $3,150	$3,151 to $15,450	Over $15,450

As you can see, those who have lower incomes may not have to pay any capital gains tax at all. For 2024, if you are a single person with an income of $47,025 or less, or married filing jointly with a household income of $94,050 or less, you could earn any amount of money investing and not owe a penny in taxes on your profits.

The very-high-income earners—those making more than $518,450 single or $583,750 married filing jointly a year—pay a 20% long-term capital gains tax rate.

For everyone in between, the long-term capital gains tax rate is 15%.

There are some exceptions and nuances to these guidelines, so, as always, consult your tax professional for your own situation.

SHORT-TERM CAPITAL GAINS TAX

If you sell an asset before you have owned it for a year, it is considered a *short-term holding* and you pay short-term capital gains tax rates on any profit.

Short-term capital gains are essentially treated the same as any other ordinary income, so the short-term tax rate is the *highest marginal tax rate* you pay on your normal income. For tax year 2024, common marginal tax rates are 22% and 24% (but could be as low as 10% or as high as 37%),[69] so if you try to play the investing game with a short-term mindset and are in those tax brackets, you could lose an extra 7% or 9% even when you win! Those tax bills can really add up over time to sap your total returns.

Remember our Dogs of the Dow investing strategy? Remember how I said to hold on to each dog for at least one year? Short-term capital gains tax is the reason. While your investment returns will rarely be materially different by selling a couple days later, if you hold your investment for one full year, your tax rate goes from the short-term rates to the long-term rates, which is usually beneficial.

Let me reiterate an important point: Any time you plan to sell an investment, *make sure you've talked with your tax professional* to understand the implications. The last thing you want is an unexpected tax bill!

ALLANISM

You do not make or lose money in the stock market unless you sell your stocks.

———————

MUST-KNOW FACT 38
Even the longest of long-term investors don't hold on forever.

One of the funny things about the stock market is that every time one person buys, another sells, and both think they are astute.
WILLIAM FEATHER, PUBLISHER AND AUTHOR

———————
—————

After you've bought some stocks and really gotten your portfolio rolling, you may start to ask yourself: "How will I know when it's time to sell a stock?"

The reason I intentionally haven't addressed that question thus far is that *The Wannabe Investor* is geared toward helping people learn how to *invest* rather than how to *trade*. There's a big difference. Traders try to profit by hopping in and out of stocks quickly to take advantage of relatively short-term price changes. Investors carefully pick companies that they believe in and hold on to their stocks for the long haul, ignoring (as much as they can) the inevitable short-term turbulence.

There's a reason that you've never heard anyone call themselves a "day investor."

But even long-term investors will at some point hit the sell button. Just look at the portfolio of Warren Buffett, who famously quipped that his "favorite holding period is forever." He's a witty billionaire, that Buffett, but he and his portfolio managers at Berkshire Hathaway sell shares and even close entire positions regularly. For example, in 2022 alone, Berkshire sold or reduced its stake in Verizon, AbbVie, Bristol-Myers Squibb, Royalty Pharma, STORE Capital, and Wells Fargo.

Obviously, Buffet and his lieutenants liked those stocks enough at one point to buy them. And Berkshire still has plenty of cash on hand that it could make purchases with. So why would he sell? Perhaps because the reasons he bought those stocks no longer apply. This, in my view, is the best reason to sell a stock. Situations change. Consumer preferences shift. Competitive advantages erode. If the argument you made to yourself to justify a stock buy no longer convinces you, and you can't find an equally compelling new argument, it's okay to head for the exit.

Another good reason can be as simple as this: you see a more profitable long-term opportunity, and you need money to invest in it. Obviously, I'm not encouraging you to jump from fad to fad pursuing the next hot stock. But if you don't see much growth opportunity left in one of your investments, it's entirely reasonable to trade it in for a more promising one.

Now, some folks will advise investors to use a strategy called *tax-loss harvesting* when they sell. Basically, if you sell stocks (or other assets) at a loss, you can report those losses on your taxes, and use them to cancel out some of the taxable capital gains from your winners. If you wind up with more capital losses in a year than you made in capital gains, the amount of those excess losses that you can deduct from your taxable income is capped at $3,000.[70] But if you have more than $3,000 in net losses, the tax code allows you to carry those losses forward and use them to reduce your tax bills in later tax years. (Once again, consult with your accountant about your specific situation.)

In short, you might want to sell a stock that fell in price to take advantage of a tax break, but that's a short-term-thinking reason to sell. If you have other good reasons to sell a stock while it's down, sure—don't forget to harvest your losses, too. But tax maneuvering on its own is not usually sufficient reason to hit the sell button—and this is why having a financial advisor to consult is essential.

Some people also suggest selling shares to rebalance your portfolio. If you happen to pick one stock that significantly outperforms the others, it can come to represent a much larger piece of your portfolio than you originally intended it to. And while that's great in some ways, it also means that if anything goes wrong for that company, it will cause you an awful lot of financial pain. Selling some shares and investing in other stocks will restore the diversification you set out to achieve.

But . . .

As much as I might want to fully recommend such a smart, cautious strategy, I can't. Allan, for one, certainly didn't use it. His Coca-Cola investment grew and grew over the decades, and he didn't sell shares to hedge his risk in case it plunged. It's now a major piece of his net worth. Warren Buffett did not intentionally put almost half of Berkshire's stock portfolio into Apple. He made a much smaller investment in the tech company, and then Apple stock grew into that massive position. Buffett let it ride. And he's still letting it ride, probably because the reasons he bought Apple still apply.

David Gardner, co-founder of The Motley Fool (which is dedicated to helping people pursue a long-term investing approach), has an adage for this: "Let your winners run." It's not a bad idea. They're usually winners for a reason.

Finally, of course, sometimes you'll sell simply because you need the money. We invest with goals in mind: to pay for someone's education, to make a down payment on a house, to retire in a bit of style and comfort. When it's time to cash out for the right reasons, it's time. That's what you were investing *for*.

I'll call back to those sage words of wisdom from Buffett one last time: "If you aren't willing to own a stock for ten years, don't even think about owning it for ten minutes." But *willing to* doesn't mean *have to*.

Go into your investments willing to hold on, but don't feel bad about selling when the time is right.

ALLANISM

Enjoy the rewards you reap from your solid investment decisions.

———————

MUST-KNOW FACT 39
You're never too young to start investing in the stock market.

Kids will be more interested in investing if they're investing in something they have a connection with.

SUSAN DZIUBINSKI, INVESTING SPECIALIST WITH MORNINGSTAR

———————

No matter what age you are when you decide you're ready to start investing, odds are that you'll wish that you had started earlier.

While Allan often reminds me that there are no "should haves," I often question why I was not financially savvy enough to begin investing in stocks in my twenties or thirties. I remember hearing about the Employee Retirement Income Security Act (ERISA), which gave us the 401(k), in 1974. Then when I was thirty-four, the company I worked for offered a 401(k) plan and I did not think I could afford to have money taken out of my paycheck, so I did not take advantage of opening this pre-tax investment fund. If only . . .

Rather than planning for my financial future, however, I focused on the monthly expenses of my life. I was far more concerned about paying down the principal on my mortgage by adding an extra $60 per month to the payment. If only I had recognized then how much those 401(k) contributions would have grown!

They say you learn two things from everyone: what to do and what *not* to do. In this case, I hope you'll learn what not to do by taking the lesson from what I should have done. (Shhhh! Please don't tell Allan I said "should have.")

While I could not turn back the clock for myself, what I did instead was to teach my children and grandchildren to begin investing much earlier in life than I did. When my son and daughter got out of school and started their careers, I encouraged them to take advantage of their employers' 401(k) plans. Luckily, they did just that.

And when my two granddaughters, Catalina and Sonya, were seven and eleven years old, respectively, I made a grandparental decision. Rather than continuing to give them toys and clothes for special occasions, I decided to begin investing in their financial futures by gifting them shares of stock. That's something you, too, can do for any of the young people in your life, and it's extremely simple to begin.

Step one was to open a *custodial brokerage account*—an account that an adult controls for a minor—for each of my granddaughters at the brokerage where I was already a client. The most critical piece of information you need to do this is the Social Security number of the child you're opening the account for. (Of course, as with almost everything we've discussed, there are pros and cons to custodial accounts, and we can't cover everything here, so do a little reading before you jump in.)

I began this stock-picking gift adventure by choosing companies I knew the girls would understand. I also wanted them to receive a tangible present each time they were gifted a share of stock. After giving it much thought, I decided to buy each of them a sterling silver charm bracelet, to which I would regularly add charms representing the companies whose stocks they were given.

The first time they were presented with these unusual gifts, I explained to each of them that the purpose was for them to receive presents from me that would make them part owners of companies with which they were familiar.

"These are gifts you will never outgrow," I told them. "On the contrary, these gifts will keep growing for both of you!"

Now if you're questioning whether a seven-year-old or even an eleven-year-old can really comprehend the idea of owning a piece of a company, you may not be giving kids the credit they deserve. Admittedly, I wondered the same thing until two weeks after Catalina and Sonya received their first share of stock: Disney. (They each received a Minnie Mouse charm!)

While neither of these girls had ever been to the Magic Kingdom, their gifts did have a certain magical effect: Sonya became a bit *enchanted* with the idea of her first stock and assessing how it might grow. Two weeks after celebrating her eleventh birthday, she shared with me what seemed to be expert knowledge about her newly gifted stock. "Our Disney stocks are growing!" she said excitedly.

"I'm so glad to hear that, honey," I replied. "However, how do you know?"

Confidently, Sonya told me, "When Catalina and I went trick-or-treating last night, we saw so many kids wearing Disney costumes!"

Talk about a brilliant comment from a new investor!

ALLANISM

**Investing in stocks is like planting a tree—
it takes time, patience, and nurturing. In time,
it can grow into a fruitful source of wealth.**

———————

MUST-KNOW FACT 40
You're never too old to start investing in the stock market.

Endurance is patience concentrated.
THOMAS CARLYLE, HISTORIAN AND ESSAYIST

———————

When Stella was ninety-one, a friend told her, "Ninety is the new sixty." That comment, which you might expect her to meet with a smile, instead set off alarm bells.

For the prior fifty years, Stella had kept all of her money in a savings account. She knew that the interest her bank paid had never kept up with inflation. However, she had calculated many times that if her money grew at even a minuscule rate, it would allow her to maintain a comfortable lifestyle until she was in her mid-eighties.

Now, however, she was past her eighties altogether, and the idea that ninety was the new sixty made her panic! Still in good health for her age, she realized she really could conceivably live another ten to fifteen years, in which case she might outlive the money she had so carefully set aside.

The nonagenarian wondered if she should adjust her financial strategy—and that she did, after hearing from a friend whose stock investments had averaged 6% annual gains during the prior decade. That, Stella knew, was a lot better than the measly 1% she was earning in her savings account. After giving it much thought, at age ninety-one, she asked that friend to help her open a brokerage account. She then funded the account with a quarter of the money in her savings account: $100,000.

While Stella knew nothing about how to buy stocks, her friend passed on three rules for investing that she habitually followed:

Rule 1: Invest no more than 10 percent of your portfolio in one stock.

Rule 2: Diversify your portfolio by investing in multiple stocks and business sectors.

Rule 3: Plan to keep the stocks for a minimum of ten years.

(Gosh, I hope those rules sound familiar by now.)

Stella took those three suggestions, and on October 2, 2013, she asked her friend to help her buy $10,000 of shares in each of ten companies.

In 2023, Stella turned 101! Check out Table 14 to see the prices Stella bought at on October 2, 2013, the prices they closed at ten years later, and her resulting profits and losses. (To keep the numbers simple, we are ignoring dividends, and some numbers may be rounded.)

Table 14. Stella's profit/loss after ten years

Company	Purchase Price	Shares Purchased	Price after 10 Years	Value after 10 years	Profit/ Loss
Aflac	$31.60	316	$76.47	$24,199	$14,199
Apple	$15.26	655	$173.00	$113,368	$103,368
Boeing	$100.00	100	$188.00	$18,800	$8,800
IBM	$140.00	71	$117.00	$8,357	-$1,643
CVS	$69.10	145	$44.57	$6,450	-$3,550
ExxonMobil	$55.74	179	$116.00	$20,811	$10,811
Gap	$40.86	245	$10.62	$2,599	-$7,401
Microsoft	$28.41	352	$321.00	$112,988	$102,988
Prudential Financial	$52.48	191	$93.38	$17,793	$7,793
Tesla	$12.06	829	$251.60	$208,624	$198,624
TOTAL				$533,990	$433,990

Ten years after Stella patiently let her ten stocks grow, seven of them had increased in value to a whopping total of $446,584! Three of her stocks, however, dropped to a combined loss of $12,594. Her net profit was $433,990. In other words, her initial $100,000 investment increased by 433% to $533,990!

Stella's results just go to show that you are never too old to start investing.

Stella is still holding on to her stocks. Why? Because she still believes in the companies she picked. And a centenarian has more reason than most to see the value of the primary piece of advice I've offered in this book: When you're investing, *think long term*.

ALLANISM

Just as you choose a mate, buy a stock that you intend to keep long term!

———————

Conclusion: Now It's Up to You

Give a man a fish, and you feed him for a day.
Teach him to fish, and you feed him for a lifetime.
ANNE ISABELLA THACKERAY RITCHIE, AUTHOR OF *MRS. DYMOND*

———————

As you transition from wannabe to first-time investor, remember these principles:

1. Investing is a journey of continuous learning. Each time you decide to invest, first do your homework by thoroughly researching the stock, ETF, index fund, or other financial vehicle.

2. Before pressing that "buy" button on your brokerage account, ask yourself if the investment fits your risk appetite, financial goals, and time horizon. These considerations will help you make solid decisions throughout your investment journey.

3. Diversify your investments by spreading them across various sectors and asset classes. Doing so will lower your risk and give your portfolio added resilience against market fluctuations.

4. Consistently monitor your investments to make sure they are aligned with your financial objectives. If you manage your own investments, get an objective perspective from a professional advisor annually.

5. Stay logical when investing in the stock market. Manage your emotions, such as fear (e.g., panic selling) and greed (e.g., buying more of an overvalued stock even though you already have favorable returns).

6. When investing, keep a long-term perspective based on your time horizon.

7. Integrate the invaluable virtues of patience and perseverance into your investing style.

8. Remind yourself of the benefits of compound growth. It will truly show its power over the long term.

By embracing these eight principles, you will be embarking on your investment journey with confidence.

The next step is for you to *commit* to practicing sound investment strategies. The Investment Commitment that follows was created to help you do just that. Following each of the eighteen investment practices below will put you in the best position possible to pick up the "fishing rod" that I am passing to you so that you, too, can begin your investing journey.

If you have a question or comment, I invite you to email me at questions@TheWannabeInvestor.com.

My Investment Commitment

1. If my employer offers a tax-advantaged retirement plan, I will contribute the highest percentage of my income that my company agrees to match each year. If my employer does not offer a retirement plan, I will open and fund a Roth or traditional IRA (consulting my tax advisor about what is best for me).

2. Before investing in stocks, I will build up an emergency fund sufficient to cover my living expenses for three to six months.

3. Before I invest in any financial vehicle or asset, I will evaluate the projected return on investment to ensure that it is greater than the rate of inflation.

4. Before I invest in a stock, I will assess whether it is a growth stock or a value stock.

5. Before I invest in a company, I will evaluate its business sector with an eye toward ensuring I maintain a diversified portfolio.

6. Before I invest in stocks, I will research them to assess if they are compatible with my risk tolerance.

7. When I buy dividend-paying stocks, I will have the dividends automatically reinvested to take full advantage of the power of compound growth.

8. Before I invest in a company's stock, I'll make sure that the business is properly managed, that it has an economic moat, and that it has adequate financial resources.

9. Before I begin my stock investing journey, I will determine if the best approach for me will be to manage my own investments, work with a financial advisor, use a robo-advisor, or employ a combination of those approaches.

10. I will practice on a virtual trading platform before I start risking my own hard-earned money.

11. I will open a brokerage account with a reputable brokerage firm.

12. I will create a stock shopping list so that when I have money to invest, I'll be ready with options.

13. Before I buy a stock, I will ask myself why I'm buying it. Am I acting because someone told me that it's a hot stock, or am I buying it because it was on my stock shopping list and is now in the "buy" range I have earmarked?

14. Before I invest in a stock, I will assess it from a technical or fundamental analysis standpoint to see if it is overbought, oversold, or if it is in my "buy" zone.

15. I will refrain from panic selling when the stock market experiences a crash or a correction. Instead, I will remind myself that if I take a long-term approach, most of that short-term noise will eventually even out, and by holding on, I'll be in the market and able to benefit when it recovers.

16. As I continue to invest, I will determine if I prefer the dollar-cost averaging strategy or the lump-sum investing approach.

17. As a responsible investor, I will stay apprised of the amount of taxes I will owe based on the performance of my investments.

18. If there are important minors in my life, I will consider setting up portfolio accounts for them, so that I can buy them stock as gifts that will keep on giving—and growing.

———
———

Acknowledgments

Thank you to Allan, my language-of-investing guru and Ahuvi; to Shirley J., who raised my level of awareness about what wannabe investors really want to know before they dip their toes in the stock market; to Mathew Schwartz, a terrific editor; to Steve S., who constructively critiqued this manuscript from a seasoned investor's perspective; to Lewl Shiferaw, my adopted nephew and beta reader; to Paul Haggerty, who so graciously reviewed the manuscript before it went to press; to Howard Grossman, who gave this book a face by designing its cover; and to Karin Wiberg and Jenni Hart at Clear Sight Books, who helped me get this book in focus and into the world for Soncata Press.

Notes

[1] The Economist Group, "The New American Investor: Finding Confidence in Their Financial Future," 2022. While the number of Americans invested in the market fluctuates, it has hovered around 60 percent since the 1990s, and the figure includes individual stocks as well as stocks held in a mutual fund or retirement account.

[2] Phil Laut, *Money Is My Friend: Eliminate Your Financial Fears—and Take Your First Steps to Financial Freedom!* Ballantine Books, 1999.

[3] U.S. Bureau of Labor Statistics, Economic News Release: Table A-12. Unemployed persons by duration of unemployment, accessed 20 January 2024.

[4] Erica Sandberg, "Survey: More Americans are carrying debt, and many of them don't know their APRs," Bankrate, 10 January 2023.

[5] Elizabeth Gravier, "Sallie Krawcheck: Building an emergency fund before paying off your credit card debt is bad advice," CNBC, 29 December 2022.

[6] Marley Jay, "Inflation is driving up consumer credit card debt by billions of dollars," NBC News, 12 September 2023.

[7] National Financial Educators Council, "Financial Illiteracy Cost Americans $1,506 in 2023," accessed 8 January 2024.

[8] "How many states require students to take a personal finance course before graduating from high school?" Next Gen Personal Finance, 12 February 2020, updated 1 August 2023.

[9] Jordan Rosenfeld, "Financial Literacy Around the World: Top 10 Countries and the US," Yahoo! Finance, 20 April 2022.

[10] National Conference of State Legislators, "Financial Literacy 2023 Legislation," accessed 4 December 2023.

[11] Liz Knueven, Rickie Houston, and Tessa Campbell, "Average stock market return over the past 10 years," *Business Insider*, 18 September 2023.

[12] Adam S. Minsky, "If You Work and Have Student Loans, These New Benefits Could Help," *Forbes*, 4 January 2024.

[13] Rachel Carey, "Financial Confidence in the US," Unbiased, 5 October 2023.

[14] The Economist Group, *The New American Investor*.

[15] "The History of 'Bull' and 'Bear' Markets," *Merriam-Webster.com Dictionary*, accessed 4 December 2023.

[16] Kadi Arula, "What Is a Bear Market?" Finbold, 7 December 2021.

[17] David Zeiler, "What's the Difference Between a Bear Market and a Recession?" *Money Morning*, 9 April 2020.

[18] Brian Beers, "Cash Dividends vs. Stock Dividends," Investopedia, 18 January 2022.

[19] Jason Hall, "How Are Dividends Taxed?" The Motley Fool, 30 November 2023.

[20] Adam Hayes, "What Does Ex-Dividend Mean, and What Are the Key Dates?" Investopedia, 21 November 2023.

[21] Chris Clark, "How much money do I need to live entirely off dividends?" Moneywise, 28 September 2022.

[22] Joshua Kennon, "Reinvesting Dividends vs. Not Reinvesting Dividends: A 50-Year Case Study of Coca-Cola Stock," joshuakennon.com, 28 July 2012.

[23] Prakash Kolli, "Dividend Millionaire – Grace Groner," Dividend Power website, 27 September 2023.

[24] James Chen, "Compound: What It Means, Calculation, Example," Investopedia, 26 April 2022.

[25] Statista Research Department, "NYSE and NASDAQ monthly number of listed companies comparison 2018–2023, by domicile," Statista, 22 May 2023.

[26] David Rodeck, "10 Best Material Stocks of December 2023," *Forbes*, 1 December 2023.

[27] Noel Randewich, "Facebook, Alphabet Shifted in Sector Classification System," Reuters, 11 January 2018.

[28] Phil Mackintosh, "Splitting Stocks Changes Them Fundamentally," Nasdaq website, 24 September 2020.

[29] Street Authority, "6 Traits of a Wide-Moat Stock," Nasdaq website, 24 March 2015.

[30] Location Facts, Walmart website, accessed 9 January 2024.

[31] Daniel Kline, "Costco and Target Have a Huge Edge Over Walmart (It's Not Price)," TheStreet, 25 April 2022.

[32] Samuel Smith, "Amazon Stock: Powerful Moat and Undervalued," TipRanks, 8 March 2022.

[33] Abhinav Davuluri, "We've Upgraded Apple's Fair Value Estimate and Economic Moat," Morningstar, 24 January 2023.

[34] VanEck, "Moat Stocks Take Early Lead in 2023," Seeking Alpha, 9 February 2023.

[35] Harry Burman, "What Is Berkshire Hathaway's Competitive Advantage (Moat)?" Value Investors Central, accessed 9 January 2024.

[36] Jeff Sommer, "Mutual Funds That Consistently Beat the Market? Not One of 2,132." *The New York Times*, 2 December 2022.

[37] "How SPY Reinvented Investing: The Story of the First US ETF," State Street Global Advisors, 12 January 2023.

[38] Dinah Wisenberg Brin, "Active Funds Failed to Beat Passive Peers in 2022: Morningstar," Think Advisor, 1 March 2023.

[39] Matt Krantz, "More Than a Third of S&P 500 Stocks Get Kicked Out in Nine Years," Investor's Business Daily, 6 September 2023.

[40] S&P Dow Jones Indices, *Dow Jones Averages Methodology*, December 2023.

[41] Tim Vipond, "IPO Process," Corporate Finance Institute (CFI) website, accessed 11 January 2024.

[42] Luisa Beltran, "IPO outlook: After a boom and bust in recent years, 2023 may be the year unicorns Stripe, Chime, and Instacart list shares," *Fortune*, 20 December 2022.

[43] Jackie Lam, "History of Credit Cards: When Were Credit Cards Invented?" SoFi, 10 May 2022.

[44] "How Law Enforcement Catches Cryptocurrency Crimes," Friedman & Nemecek, LLC website, 27 February 2019.

[45] "SEC Charges Genesis and Gemini for the Unregistered Offer and Sale of Crypto Asset Securities through the Gemini Earn Lending Program," US Securities and Exchange Commission press release, 12 January 2023.

[46] Lyle Daly, "How Many Cryptocurrencies Are There?" The Motley Fool, 27 June 2022.

[47] Nathaniel Popper, "Lost Passwords Lock Millionaires Out of Their Bitcoin Fortunes," *The New York Times*, 12 January 2021.

[48] Jessica Dickler, "75 percent of Americans are winging it when it comes to their financial future," CNBC, 2 April 2019.

[49] "Americans Are More Confident About Their Retirement Savings Now Versus Three Years Ago Pre-Trump, According to the Invest in You Savings Survey," CNBC news release, 1 April 2019.

[50] David Zeiler, "How the 2008 Stock Market Crash Compares to 2016," *Money Morning*, 29 January 2016.

[51] US Securities and Exchange Commission, "Commission Interpretation Regarding Standard of Conduct for Investment Advisers," effective 12 July 2019.

[52] Check Your Investment Professional page, US Securities and Exchange Commission website.

[53] Mission and Fiduciary Oath page, The National Association of Personal Financial Advisors website.

[54] Kevin Voigt, "Fee-Only Financial Planner vs. Fee-Based: What's the Difference?" NerdWallet, 30 January 2023.

[55] "Portfolio Management vs. Financial Planning: Know the Difference," Investopedia, 8 October 2022.

[56] Lance Cothern, "13 Questions to Ask When Interviewing a Financial Advisor," Money Under 30, 14 November, 2023.

[57] Ria & Qing, "The Story Behind the First Ever Robo-Advisor," Aqumon, 2 April 2019.

[58] Frank Chaparro, "Betterment, the investing startup that's attracting $12 million a day, is now valued at $1 billion in private market trading," *Business Insider Nederland*, 19 October 2017.

[59] James Burton, "The Dawn of the 'Bionic Advisor'," Wealth Professional, 17 May 2018.

[60] Michael Torrence, "FOMO: Fear vs. Opportunity," Alpha Wealth Funds website, 28 July 2022.

[61] Kadi Arula, "What Is Fundamental Analysis?" Finbold, 15 August 2022.

[62] Benjamin Graham, *The Intelligent Investor: The Definitive Book on Value Investing*, Harper & Brothers, 1949.

[63] Dion Rabouin, "The world's most owned stocks," Axios, 14 June 2019.

[64] Carl Engelking, "Is Dollar-Cost Averaging Better Than Lump-Sum Investing?" Northwestern Mutual website, 13 July 2021.

[65] Gordon Scott, "Dogs of the Dow: Definition, List of Stocks, Performance," Investopedia, 31 August 2023.

[66] Robert Farrington, "Dogs of the Dow: Is This Strategy a Winner?" The College Investor, 2 May 2023.

[67] "2022 Dogs of the Dow Performance Tables," Dogs of the Dow website, accessed 17 January 2024, used with permission.

[68] "26 CFR 601.602: Tax forms and instructions," IRS website, accessed 15 January 2024.

[69] "IRS provides tax inflation adjustments for tax year 2024," IRS, 9 November 2023.

[70] "Topic no. 409, Capital gains and losses," IRS website, accessed 15 January 2024.

Recommended Resources

Whether you prefer reading or listening, below are resources to keep your wannabe investor education going! I've read, enjoyed, and learned from all the books listed here, and I've listed some terrific investing podcasts I listen to regularly. Enjoy!

Books

Abdali, Naved, *Investing Hopes, Hypes & Heartbreaks: The Game Is Rigged and Is Rigged in Your Favor*, Rosehurst Publishing, 2021.

Bogle, John C., *The Little Book of Common Sense Investing: The Only Way to Guarantee Your Fair Share of Stock Market Returns*, Wiley, 2017.

Cagan, Michele, *Investing 101: From Stocks and Bonds to ETFs and IPOs, An Essential Primer on Building a Profitable Portfolio*, Adams Media, 2016.

Carlson, Charles B., *Winning with the Dow's Losers: Beat the Market with Underdog Stocks*, Harper Business, 2003.

Collins, J L, *The Simple Path to Wealth: Your Road Map to Financial Independence and a Rich, Free Life*, CreateSpace Independent Publishing Platform, 2016.

Cramer, James J., *Jim Cramer's Get Rich Carefully*, Blue Rider Press, 2013.

Forbes, Steve; Lewis, Nathan; Ames, Elizabeth, *Inflation: What It Is, Why It's Bad, and How to Fix It*, Encounter Books, 2022.

Graham, Benjamin; Zweig, Jason, *The Intelligent Investor: The Definitive Book on Value Investing*, rev. ed., Harper Business, 2006.

Hagstrom, Robert G., *The Warren Buffett Way*, 3rd ed., Wiley, 2013.

Kiyosaki, Robert T., *Rich Dad's Guide to Investing: What the Rich Invest in, That the Poor and Middle Class Do Not!*, Plata Publishing, 2012.

Krantz, Matt, *Fundamental Analysis for Dummies*, 3rd ed., For Dummies, 2023.

Lowry, Erin, *Broke Millennial Takes On Investing: A Beginner's Guide to Leveling Up Your Money*, TarcherPerigee, 2019.

Lynch, Peter, *One Up on Wall Street: How to Use What You Already Know to Make Money in the Market*, Simon & Schuster, 2000.

Malkiel, Burton G., *A Random Walk Down Wall Street: The Time-Tested Strategy for Successful Investing*, W. W. Norton & Company, 2020.

O'Neil, William J., *How to Make Money in Stocks: A Winning System in Good Times or Bad*, McGraw Hill, 2009.

Pabrai, Mohnish, *The Dhandho Investor: The Low-Risk Value Method to High Returns*, Wiley, 2009.

Payne, Charles, *Unstoppable Prosperity*, Paradigm Direct, LLC, 2019.

Penn, A.Z, *Technical and Fundamental Analysis for Beginners*, 2 in 1 edition, self-published, 2023.

Pisani, Bob, *Shut Up & Keep Talking: Lessons on Life & Investing from the Floor of the New York Stock Exchange*, Harriman House, 2022.

Rockefeller, Barbara, *Technical Analysis for Dummies*, 4th ed., For Dummies, 2019.

Siegel, Jeremy, *Stocks for the Long Run: The Definitive Guide to Financial Market Returns and Long-Term Investment Strategies*, 6th ed., McGraw Hill, 2022.

Templeton, Lauren C.; Phillips, Scott, *Investing the Templeton Way: The Market-Beating Strategies of Value Investing's Legendary Bargain Hunter*, McGraw Hill, 2008.

Town, Phil, *Rule #1: The Simple Strategy for Successful Investing in Only 15 Minutes a Week!*, Currency, 2007.

Villermin, Luke, *On Your Mark, Get Set, INVEST: A Kid's Guide to Saving Money, Spending Wisely, and Investing in the Stock Market*, Play Later Publishing, 2023.

Villermin, Luke, *A Teenager's Guide to Investing in the Stock Market: Invest Hard Now, Play Hard Later*, Play Later Publishing, 2020.

Podcasts

Fast Money (https://www.cnbc.com/2018/03/01/fast-money-podcast.html). Episode releases: Weekdays. Average episode duration: 45 minutes.

Invest Like the Best (https://investorfieldguide.com/podcast/). Episode releases: Tuesdays. Average episode duration: 60 minutes.

InvestED (https://www.ruleoneinvesting.com/podcast/). Episode releases: Tuesdays. Average episode duration: 30 minutes.

Motley Fool Money (https://www.fool.com/podcasts/motley-fool-money/). Episode releases: Daily. Average episode duration: 40 minutes.

The Rich Dad Radio Show (https://www.richdad.com/radio). Episode releases: Wednesdays. Average episode duration: 45 to 60 minutes.

Stacking Benjamins (https://www.stackingbenjamins.com/podcast). Episode releases: Every Monday, Wednesday, and Friday. Average episode duration: 60 minutes.

Index

About the Author

ANN MARIE SABATH founded At Ease Inc., a New York-based business consulting firm, in 1987. During her thirty-three years as its president, she and her team assisted more than 200,000 professionals, many of them representing Fortune 500 companies, in increasing their organizations' profits.

Sabath has authored ten previous books intended to help individuals learn how to become masters of their own success. The *Wall Street Journal*, CNBC, CNN, *USA Today*, and numerous other media organizations have recognized her books and concepts.

Other Books by Ann Marie Sabath

What Self-Made Millionaires Do That Most People Don't
Courting Business: 101 Ways for Accelerating Business Relationships
One Minute Manners: Quick Solutions to the Most Awkward Situations You'll Ever Face at Work
Business Etiquette: 101 Ways to Do Business with Charm & Savvy
Everybody Has a Book Inside of Them: How to Bring It Out
Business Casual: What to Wear to Work If You Want to Get Ahead
Business Etiquette in Brief
International Business Etiquette: Asia & the Pacific Rim
International Business Etiquette: Europe
International Business Etiquette: Latin America

Milton Keynes UK
Ingram Content Group UK Ltd.
UKHW050705270324
440147UK00019B/310/J

9 798989 857418